LOST SHIPYARDS OF THE TYNE

'They build ships here to perfection as to strength and firmness, and to bear the sea.'
Daniel Defoe, 1727, after visiting the Tyne

Ron French and Ken Smith

Tyne Bridge Publishing

Acknowledgments

The authors wish to thank the following people for their kind help in the preparation of this book: John Dobson, Joe Clarke, Jim Cuthbert, Derek Henderson, Dick Keys, Alan Myers, George Coltman, Noreen Coltman, Alan Mather, Fred McCabe, George Andrews, Ian Wilson, Bob Koch, Tommy Peebles, David Baines, Ray Marshall, the staff of South Tyneside Libraries Local Studies, and the staff of Newcastle City Libraries Local Studies.

Tyne Bridge Publishing would like to thank Swan Hunter (Tyneside) Ltd; Bill Jackson, Shields Ferry; Tyne & Wear Archives; Tyne & Wear Museums; H.S. Thorne.

Photographs ©Newcastle Libraries unless otherwise indicated.

Front cover: the battleship HMS *Superb*, completed at the Armstrong Whitworth Yard, Elswick, 1909, moves down the Tyne, past the Swing Bridge.

Back cover: *Esso Northumbria*, Swan Hunter, April 1969.

Frontispiece: detail from 'Shipbuilding on the River Tyne … 1842' possibly by J.W. Carmichael (private collection).

Cover design by A.V. Flowers

Lost Shipyards of the Tyne ©Ron French, Ken Smith, 2004

ISBN: 978 1 85795 122 6

Published by
City of Newcastle upon Tyne
Education & Libraries
Newcastle Libraries, Information & Lifelong Learning Service
Tyne Bridge Publishing
2004, revised reprint 2007

www.tynebridgepublishing.co.uk

Printed by Elanders Hindson, North Tyneside

Other maritime history books available from Tyne Bridge Publishing

Mauretania Pride of the Tyne, Ken Smith, ISBN: 978 1 85795 043 4

Palmers of Jarrow, Jim Cuthbert and Ken Smith, ISBN: 978 185795 196 7

Swan Hunter: the Pride and the Tears, Ian Rae and Ken Smith, ISBN: 978 1 85795 106 6

Tales from the Tyne, Dick Keys and Ken Smith, ISBN: 978 1 85795 158 5

Tall Ships on the Tyne, Dick Keys and Ken Smith, ISBN: 978 185795 137 0

Turbinia: the Story of Charles Parsons and his Ocean Greyhound, Ken Smith, ISBN: 978 1 85795 077 9

Contents

The Gaddy and Lamb wooden shipbuilding yard at Tyne Main, Gateshead. The firm was established before 1840 and launched a variety of sailing vessels, including full-rigged ships and barques. Gaddy and Lamb was one of the longest surviving wooden yards on the Tyne.
See page 67.

Men and Iron

On February 21 1814 a steam paddle boat was launched from the South Shore at Gateshead into the River Tyne. Named the *Tyne Steam Packet*, she is likely to have been the first steam-driven vessel built on the river. It would also be claimed that she was the first steamboat to carry on passenger traffic in English waters.

The wooden-hulled craft naturally caused a considerable stir among the people of Tyneside when on 19 May of that year she steamed down the river, carrying passengers between Newcastle and Shields. It was the Newcastle mayor's traditional river parade day, known as Barge Day.

'Being Ascension Day, it joined the procession of barges etc and was a great novelty,' wrote one observer. According to the *Newcastle Chronicle* the *Tyne Steam Packet* was the 'principal novelty of the day' as she steamed along the river, 'greatly outstripping' the Newcastle Corporation procession 'by the rapidity of its motion'.

The *Chronicle* continued to wax lyrical over the steamboat: 'The velocity with which it moves through the water, when favoured by the tide, is very great, having run from Shields to this town (Newcastle), we understand, in less than an hour. Against the tide, its motion, of course is not so rapid; but even thus impeded it appears to move at the rate of three or four miles an hour.'

A few weeks later the *Chronicle* reported that the *Tyne Steam Packet* had begun a regular passenger service between Newcastle and Shields. In celebration of the new service 'a number of gentlemen proceeded in the vessel to Shields, where the party was regaled with an excellent dinner on board'. They then returned to Newcastle Quay where 'a number of ladies joined the party'. From there, the vessel steamed up river to Lemington on an early evening cruise. 'In this latter voyage, tea and other refreshments were served up; and numerous dances, into which the company entered with great spirit, contributed to the novel festivity of the day.'

During Tyneside's Race Week, ending on 25 June 1814, it appears there was considerable demand for pleasure trips in the boat. Best cabins were advertised at one shilling and 'second cabins' at six pence.

The *Tyne Steam Packet* was later renamed *Perseverance* to

To be SOLD by private Contract,
A NEW VESSEL on the Stocks, ready to launch, admeasures 102 Tons and 21-94ths, is well built of the best Materials. For further Particulars, enquire of Jonathan Brown, South Shore, Gateshead, where the Vessel now stands; or of Mr Wm Winn, Quayside, Newcastle.
Gateshead, 15th March, 1814.

An advertisement for a ship built on the South Shore, Gateshead, 1814.

distinguish her from two other paddle steamers which joined the passenger service. However, the three steamboats did not make money and were eventually laid up.

In 1816 a Joseph Price of Gateshead bought the vessels and re-introduced the river passenger service, but again without success. Price looked around for an alternative use for his vessels and in 1818 began using them to tow sailing vessels in and out of the Tyne. They thus became distant forerunners of the modern-day tug. It was not too long before other steamers were employed on the river in this way.

The new form of marine propulsion led to other developments. In 1823, a 63ft-long paddle steamer, named the *Rapid*, was built on the South Shore, Gateshead. Joseph Shield, a Tyne shipping agent, placed her on a coastal service between Newcastle Quay and London. However, on her maiden voyage from the Tyne the vessel broke down off Whitby. The next year Shield tried to start the service again and this time the *Rapid* successfully reached London in 59 hours and made the trip back to the Tyne in 60. Soon other steamships began linking the Tyne with London and ports such as Leith in Scotland.

A ship under repair on the Tyne around 1860.

All these early paddle steamers had hulls made from wood. Indeed, wooden shipbuilding had existed on the Tyne for centuries. This had been given its initial impetus by the need to carry coal and other cargoes from the river.

Repair of coal-carrying vessels went hand in hand with the development of ship construction. The shipwrights who mended vessels were naturally capable of building them and ships to carry the coal were certainly needed. Shipbuilding seems to have been well-established by the early 17th century when a shipwrights' company or guild was founded in Newcastle.

It is in this century that the names of shipwrights emerge from the records. For example, a Thomas Wrangham seems to have been a prosperous Newcastle shipbuilder for part of this period. He died in 1689 at the age of 42 and his memorial stone in the former All Hallows Church in the city recorded that he 'built five and forty sail of ships'. Wrangham's yard may have been in the St Lawrence area, perhaps near the mouth of the Ouseburn, but there is no definite indication of this. It may possibly have been at St Peter's, a little further down river. There is no doubt there were many other shipwrights who engaged in building as well as repair work.

By the early 18th Century Daniel Defoe was writing of the Tyne that 'they build ships here to perfection'. One of the earliest recorded yards on the Tyne seems to have been that founded by Robert Wallis in c.1729 below the Lawe Top at South Shields. Wallis was a Freeman of Newcastle, his father having been a shipwright before him. The trade often ran in

An advertisement from the Newcastle Courant, 1814, advertises a yard for sale. It was almost certainly the Temple site at Jarrow.

families. Wallis had to contend with strong opposition from Newcastle Corporation who sought to restrict shipbuilding to the Newcastle area. A legal battle followed, with Wallis eventually winning the right to continue launching vessels at South Shields. However, research indicates that he was not the first person to build ships there. Robert Wallis's yard died with him in 1781, but his sons developed a shiprepair business.

The second half of the 18th century saw the establishment on the river of major yards capable of launching large-sized ocean-going sailing ships. Many substantial vessels were built by the firm of William Rowe at St Peter's, Newcastle, between 1756 and 1810. His yard was situated on the present-day site of St Peter's Marina and its housing

Some early Tyne wooden shipbuilding yards and two
yards which pioneered iron shipbuilding on the river.

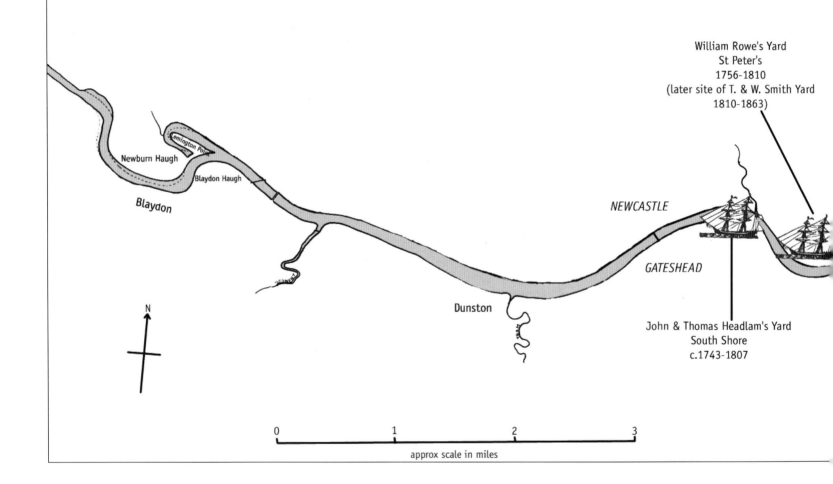

William Rowe's Yard
St Peter's
1756-1810
(later site of T. & W. Smith Yard
1810-1863)

Newburn Haugh

Blaydon Haugh

Blaydon

NEWCASTLE

GATESHEAD

Dunston

John & Thomas Headlam's Yard
South Shore
c.1743-1807

N

0   1   2   3
approx scale in miles

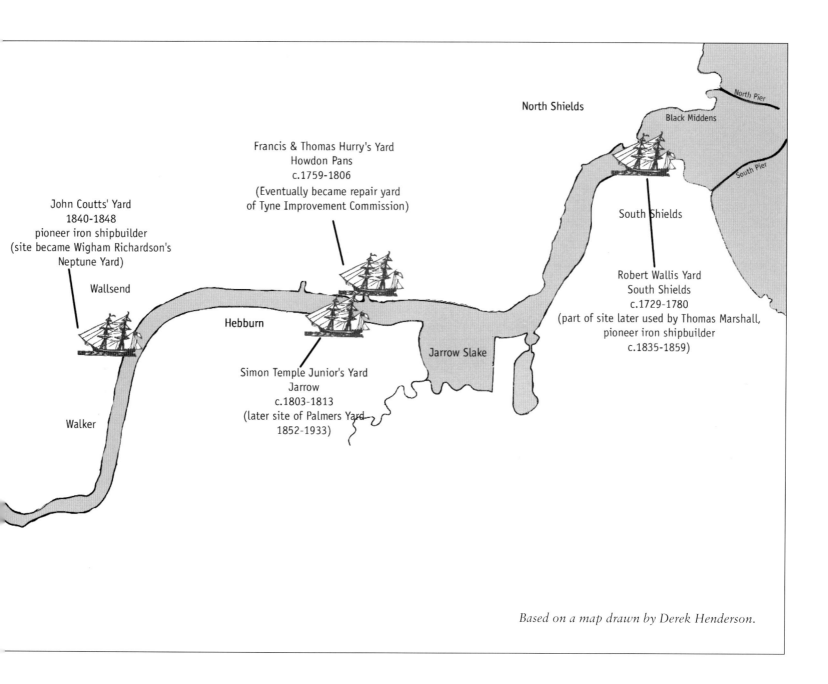

John Coutts' Yard
1840-1848
pioneer iron shipbuilder
(site became Wigham Richardson's
Neptune Yard)

Wallsend

Walker

Francis & Thomas Hurry's Yard
Howdon Pans
c.1759-1806
(Eventually became repair yard
of Tyne Improvement Commission)

Hebburn

Simon Temple Junior's Yard
Jarrow
c.1803-1813
(later site of Palmers Yard
1852-1933)

Jarrow Slake

North Shields

Black Middens

North Pier

South Pier

South Shields

Robert Wallis Yard
South Shields
c.1729-1780
(part of site later used by Thomas Marshall,
pioneer iron shipbuilder
c.1835-1859)

Based on a map drawn by Derek Henderson.

development. One of Rowe's most impressive vessels was the 150ft-long *Bucephalus*, a 32-gun frigate built for the Royal Navy, which was launched in 1808.

Other important shipbuilders in the 18th and opening few years of the 19th centuries included Francis Hurry, who ran yards at Howdon and North Shields, and the father and son, Simon Temple senior and junior, who were based at South Shields and Jarrow. Warships were among the products of Hurry's and the Temple's firms.

Francis Hurry opened his yard at Howdon in c1759 and a dry dock was installed. The site was eventually to be used as the repair yard of the Tyne Improvement Commission. Hurry, whose son Thomas joined the firm as a partner, built a considerable number of wooden warships. Among them was HMS *Argo*, completed in 1781, which was a 44-gun vessel, the largest such ship constructed on the Tyne at that date. The business launched many vessels, including merchant ships, at both Howdon and North Shields, before Francis Hurry and his son went bankrupt in 1806.

The first Temple yards were at South Shields, the firm being founded by Simon Temple Senior in c.1780. One yard was situated almost immediately down river from the present day Market Place ferry landing in the area many years later occupied by Tyne Dock Engineering, and the other up river in the East Holborn area. A yard was later opened at Jarrow, and vessels were launched there by Simon Temple Junior, during the early 1800s.

Ships built included the frigate *Cornelia*, launched in 1808. The *Newcastle Courant* reported: 'On Tuesday last, a fine new frigate was launched from the building yard of Simon Temple at Jarrow, called the *Cornelia*, to mount 32

guns. The day being remarkably fine many thousands of spectators were present.' However, the younger Temple went bankrupt in 1813.

Another early yard was operated by Headlam & Company on the South Shore, Gateshead, between c.1743 and 1807. Founded by John Headlam, and taken over by his successor, Thomas Headlam, this company is also known to have built substantially-sized ships, including the *Experiment*, of 1752, launched for the West Indies trade.

To the shipwrights who worked for these and other firms it must have seemed that timber would always be the material of their trade.

However, in 1822, eight years after the debut of the *Tyne Steam Packet*, an iron-hulled rowing boat over 30ft long was launched from Hawks' yard at Gateshead, evidence that this metal was now attracting the attention of at least one of the river's many boat and shipbuilders.

It is possible that over the next 16 years other yards on the Tyne experimented with producing iron vessels, although their efforts may have been unrecorded or forgotten in the mists of time.

What we do know, however, is that in 1839 Thomas Marshall launched a small iron river paddle steamer, named the *Star*, from his yard below the headland known as the Lawe Top at South Shields, and she seems to have been the first iron-hulled steamer built on the river.

In retrospect, we can see that Marshall had taken a momentous step, for the Tyne was destined to become one of the world's greatest centres of metal shipbuilding. The *Star* was a portent of a new era.

Iron could be shaped more easily than wood, and timber

was increasingly in short supply as British forests shrank. These were two factors which drew ambitious men towards use of iron in ship construction. In particular, those with experience in the boilermaking trade were ideally suited to building such vessels as they were accustomed to working in iron. Yet this metal would eventually give way to another. From the early 1880s onwards steel rapidly superseded iron as the preferred material.

Thomas Marshall was born in Woodhorn, Northumberland, in 1804 and originally worked as a smith and engineer. He began building ships on part of the old Robert Wallis yard below the Lawe Top in c.1835. This was one of the oldest recorded shipbuilding sites on the south bank of the Tyne.

The 1851 Census shows Marshall as living at 2 Green's Place, South Shields, with a wife, two sons and two daughters and describes him as an 'engineer' employing 100 men. His shipyard prospered and from 1842 until its closure in 1859 launched 99 iron vessels. These included five cargo ships built for Hamburg owners in 1845-1846, a series of orders which must have kept the workmen extremely busy.

By this time, Marshall had launched another trail-blazing vessel. She was the iron screw-driven steam collier *Bedlington*, the world's first steam collier. The *Bedlington*, completed in 1842, was employed on a coastal service carrying coal in wagons from the River Blyth in Northumberland to the mouth of the Tyne, where her cargo was loaded on to waiting sailing ships. She is likely to have been the first substantially-sized sea-going iron ship built on the river and was over 135ft long. The *Bedlington* sailed on her short maiden voyage in September 1842.

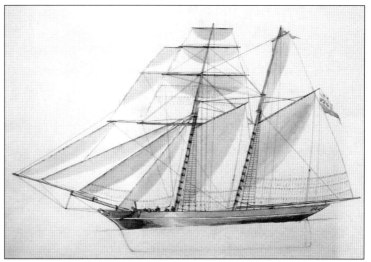

Laing Art Gallery, Tyne & Wear Museums

The Coutts-built schooner Flash, *of 1843. She is thought to have been the first iron-hulled sailing vessel launched on the North-East coast.*

By the late 1850s Thomas Marshall's yard at South Shields was becoming too small for the growing business. Marshall retired in 1859 and his sons moved the shipbuilding operation to a new yard at Willington Quay, near Wallsend, on the north bank of the Tyne. Their father died at Bensham, Gateshead, in 1864. He is one the earliest known pioneers of iron shipbuilding on the river and set the stage for greater things to come.

The location of Marshall's South Shields yard is hard to pinpoint with accuracy, but it was undoubtedly situated somewhere between Wapping Street and the Groyne below the Roman fort. Unsurprisingly, all traces of this pioneer's impressive shipbuilding endeavours have long since vanished.

Also occupying an important place among the pioneers is Aberdeenshire-born John Coutts, who in c.1842 took over a former wooden shipbuilding yard at Low Walker, Newcastle, and began constructing iron ships. Coutts had gained experience in his trade in London and Aberdeen before arriving in the North-East.

His first vessel, the 155ft-long paddle steamer *Prince Albert*, was the second substantially-sized iron ship built on the Tyne. She was launched in September 1842, the same month in which the *Bedlington* made her maiden voyage from Blyth to Shields. The *Prince Albert* was to spend much of her useful life steaming up and down the Thames carrying passengers between London and Gravesend, but may have sometimes taken trips into the coastal waters outside the Thames Estuary.

This first vessel from the Low Walker yard was followed by the *Flash*, of 1843, an iron sailing ship described as a 'clipper schooner'. She is thought to have been the earliest sailing vessel built of iron on the North-East coast.

The year 1844 witnessed the launch by Coutts of the auxiliary steam screw-driven collier *Q.E.D.*, which included the innovative feature of water ballast tanks in the vessel's double-bottomed iron hull. Like most early steamships she carried a considerable spread of sails and used her engines only when winds or tides were unfavourable.

Steam was still largely considered an auxiliary form of motive power, and vessels which used only sail were still in considerable demand. In 1845-1846, for example, the yard built no less than 14 iron sailing ships, 11 of them schooners. Not until 1847 did Coutts return to building a ship using the new form of power, the iron screw steamer *Adonis*, a fast-runner on the packet (general cargo and passengers) route between London and St Petersburg.

These were years of hard work for Coutts and his men, but they were not without their moments of enjoyment. In January 1846, for example, the *Newcastle Daily Journal* reported that 'the workmen and others in the employ of John Coutts Esq of the Tyne Iron Shipbuilding Yard were, with their wives and sweethearts, entertained on New Year's Eve in the draughting room of the establishment at Walker, which had been previously fitted up for the occasion.

'After dinner a number of appropriate toasts were given and responded to, after which dancing commenced and was kept up with great spirit until a late hour the following morning'.

John Coutts was indeed among those at the forefront of iron shipbuilding, but he was to have his problems. In 1848 he was declared bankrupt and the Low Walker yard and its machinery sold. Fortunately, within a few months he managed to have the bankruptcy annulled by selling the iron schooner *Rifleman*, the firm's 21st and last vessel.

Having regained his solvency, the following year Coutts set up in the business of shipbuilding again, this time with a partner, William Parkinson, who handled the financial side of the firm's affairs. They chose a site known as 'Willington Groins' on the northern bank of the Tyne at Willington Quay, a relatively short distance down river from Low Walker.

The new business built a number of large iron sailing vessels, including American and Australian emigrant ships. It also turned out three steamers. The firm's first vessel was the iron brigantine *Sally Gale*, of 1850, and she was followed by 13 more ships. Among them was the iron barque *Thomas Hamlin*, of 1851, which was said to be the first iron ship to

Shields Harbour in the early 19th century as depicted by J.W. Carmichael. On the right, at South Shields, is a ship on the stocks at the shipyard of the Young family, known as the West Docks. Generations of Youngs were builders and owners of wooden sailing ships between 1824 and 1871. Cuthbert, Thomas and James Young were the most prominent members of the family. The West Docks later became Readhead's shipyard.

load at the new Sunderland Dock. Her cargo of coal was bound for Calcutta.

Other major vessels were to follow. The *W.S. Lindsay*, of 1852, was a 202ft-long full-rigged iron sailing ship which eventually carried emigrants on the run to Australia. The early years at Willington Quay seem to have been happy and prosperous ones for Coutts. By 1851 he was living with his wife Margaret and five children in a large house at Picton Place near the present-day Laing Art Gallery in Newcastle.

Sadly, Coutts' partner William Parkinson died in late 1852 and within a few years the yard hit major financial problems. The shipbuilder gave up the Willington Quay business in 1856, his last vessel being the iron screw steamer *Queen Victoria*, of 1855. The firm had collapsed and he was unable to obtain new financial backing. Coutts then tried a career as a naval architect and consultant until c.1860, but had little success. It seems that his wife and family moved to London without him. Separated from them, the unlucky pioneer died in poverty at North Shields in 1862. But, like Thomas Marshall, he had begun the transformation of the Tyne into a shipbuilding river of the foremost importance.

The site of his Willington Groins yard was acquired by Palmers of Jarrow in 1860 and it remained in their ownership, under the name Howdon Yard, until 1912. It was then acquired by shipbuilders J.T. Eltringham, a company famous for constructing tugs. Today, the site has been lost under modern riverside developments, but it was situated to the east of Willington Gut and was formerly used by Press Offshore as part of its oil rig module building area.

From 1860 the land occupied by Coutts' first yard, at Low Walker, became the headquarters of another famous shipbuilder, John Wigham Richardson. He renamed it the Neptune Yard and his business went on to create many vessels. Cableships, designed for laying and repairing telegraph and telephone cables were a speciality of this yard. Neptune's first vessel of this type was the *Colonia*, delivered in 1902. Twenty-three other cableships were to follow over many years. Other important vessels included the Spanish passenger liner and troopship *Alfonso XII*, launched in 1888, and the *Hornby Grange*, one of the world's first large, refrigerated cargo ships, completed in 1890. Passenger ferries for service between the Tyne and Norway were also among the numerous craft launched.

In 1903 Wigham Richardson's company merged with C.S. Swan & Hunter of Wallsend to become Swan, Hunter & Wigham Richardson, thus forming one of the most famous shipbuilding concerns on the Tyne. The Neptune and Wallsend yards were now united in what was to become a highly successful partnership. The last ship to be launched at Neptune was the Type 22 frigate HMS *Chatham*, which slid down the ways in January 1988. At the time of writing, the jetty area of the Neptune Yard has been acquired by shiprepairers A. & P. Tyne and incorporated into their adjacent Wallsend Dry Docks. It is situated at the end of Oil Mill Road, a turning off the junction of Fisher Street and Neptune Road, Low Walker. The rest of the yard site, which is likely to be redeveloped, adjoins Fisher Street. Modern, metal gates opposite a derelict public house in Fisher Street mark the position of the main entrance to Neptune. Today, few would realise that this is the site where Coutts once launched his pioneering iron queens into the waters of the Tyne.

The launch of the tanker Matadian *at Swan Hunter & Wigham Richardson's Neptune Yard, Low Walker, Newcastle, in 1936. The yard was once the site of John Coutts' shipbuilding business. He was a pioneer of iron shipbuilding on the Tyne.*

Major Tyne shipbuilding yards of the 20th century, and some 19th century yards.

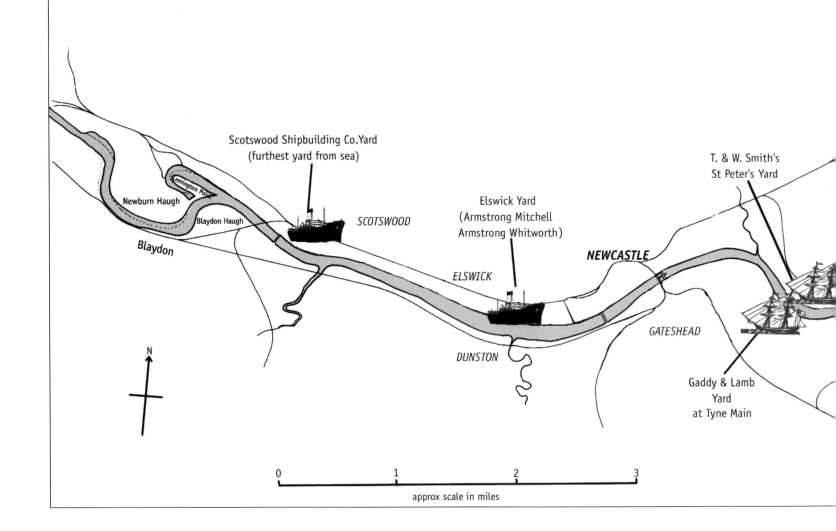

Scotsswood Shipbuilding Co.Yard
(furthest yard from sea)

T. & W. Smith's
St Peter's Yard

Elswick Yard
(Armstrong Mitchell
Armstrong Whitworth)

Newburn Haugh

Lemington Point

Blaydon Haugh

Blaydon

SCOTSWOOD

ELSWICK

NEWCASTLE

GATESHEAD

DUNSTON

Gaddy & Lamb
Yard
at Tyne Main

N

0   1   2   3

approx scale in miles

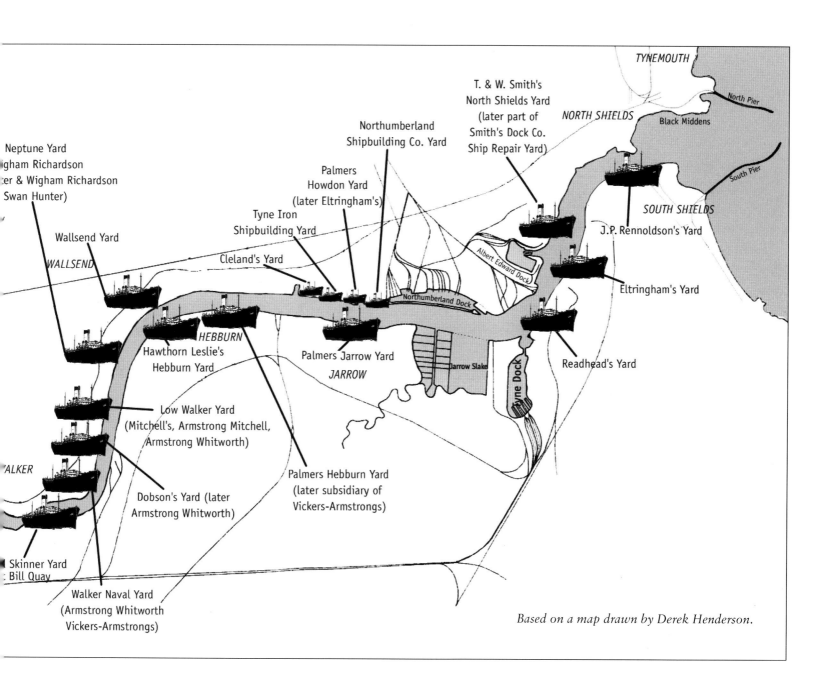

Neptune Yard
gham Richardson
er & Wigham Richardson
Swan Hunter)

Wallsend Yard

WALLSEND

Tyne Iron
Shipbuilding Yard

Cleland's Yard

Northumberland
Shipbuilding Co. Yard

Palmers
Howdon Yard
(later Eltringham's)

T. & W. Smith's
North Shields Yard
(later part of
Smith's Dock Co.
Ship Repair Yard)

TYNEMOUTH

North Pier

NORTH SHIELDS   Black Middens

South Pier

SOUTH SHIELDS

J.P. Rennoldson's Yard

Albert Edward Dock

Northumberland Dock

Eltringham's Yard

HEBBURN

Hawthorn Leslie's
Hebburn Yard

Palmers Jarrow Yard

JARROW

Jarrow Slake

Tyne Dock

Readhead's Yard

Low Walker Yard
(Mitchell's, Armstrong Mitchell,
Armstrong Whitworth)

Palmers Hebburn Yard
(later subsidiary of
Vickers-Armstrongs)

ALKER

Dobson's Yard (later
Armstrong Whitworth)

Skinner Yard
Bill Quay

Walker Naval Yard
(Armstrong Whitworth
Vickers-Armstrongs)

Based on a map drawn by Derek Henderson.

17

A Fleet of Tramp Steamers

In 1842 a young millwright and engineer named John Readhead joined Thomas Marshall's shipbuilding firm in South Shields and over the next 16 years gained valuable experience there.

Readhead was born in c.1819 in Earsdon Parish, Northumberland, and served an apprenticeship as a millwright at Earsdon Colliery. His move to the shipbuilding yard below the Lawe Top was to prove one of the most significant decisions in his life. Shortly afterwards, he was married to Susannah Richardson, of South Shields, and they went on to have four sons and a daughter.

Readhead clearly did well at Marshall's yard, for in 1859 he was appointed a manager at the firm's new shipbuilding base at Willington Quay. But despite his successful career, in 1865 he left the company to set up his own iron shipbuilding business at another site near the Lawe. He was joined in this venture by John Softley, who had also been a manager with Marshall's. Readhead and Softley's yard was located in the area where Wallis, and later Marshall, had built their ships, close to the river mouth and below the Lawe Top between the entrance to Wapping Street and the present-day Groyne.

Their first ship was the *Unus*, a small collier brig (sailing vessel) and the yard was prosperous for seven years, building 87 small vessels during this period, including paddle tugs, passenger ship tenders and Mediterranean and Black Sea traders. The year 1866 seems to have been a particularly good one, with the firm constructing no less than 11 vessels, comprising eight paddle steamers and three sailing ships. One of these was the *Lizzie Leslie*, an iron sailing barque, said to be the first ship to be classed '100 A1' at Lloyds.

The business seems to have flourished, but in 1872 the two men went their separate ways and the partnership between Readhead and Softley was dissolved.

John Readhead continued operations at the Lawe yard, although he was hampered by lack of space as the orders grew and decided to look for a new riverside base. In 1880 he therefore bought a site at West Docks, South Shields, immediately down river from Tyne Dock. The land had 1,000ft of river frontage.

The new yard featured three berths, which were later increased to four, and its first ship was the screw steamer *Jane Kelsall*, built for a North Shields owner.

Readhead's yard at West Docks went on to establish a solid reputation in the shipbuilding world, particularly for the construction of small cargo steamers. In addition, the firm had its own engine and boiler building department which provided the machinery for many of the vessels launched.

John Readhead was aided in his efforts by his four sons, who were appointed to leading positions in the company, which took the name John Readhead & Sons Ltd. One of them, James, eventually headed the business and became Sir

Beyond the ship in this picture is the site of one of the earliest shipbuilding areas on the Tyne. The location below the Lawe Top at South Shields, close to the river mouth, was used by wooden shipbuilder Robert Wallis in the 18th century, by pioneer iron shipbuilder Thomas Marshall, and by Readhead and Softley. This was Readhead's first shipyard site.

James Readhead, Bart, for his services to shipbuilding during the First World War. Two of the other sons, Robert and John, took the reins of the engine-building and foundry departments, while the youngest son, William Bell Readhead, was in charge of the drawing office and design section.

The business thrived and grew further, with one customer in particular making a key contribution to its success. Between 1878 and 1965 Readhead's built 87 cargo ships (tramp steamers) for Edward Hain and Company, of St Ives, Cornwall. It was an extraordinary number of vessels and Readhead's long association with Hain can have few parallels in shipbuilding history.

The Cornish shipowners were without doubt the mainstay of the order books for many years. All the Hain steamers had names beginning with the Cornish prefix 'Tre', the first vessel launched in this fleet from Readhead's being the *Trewidden*, ordered in 1878 from the Lawe yard.

But other companies also placed many orders with Readhead's, including the Strick Line, which between 1928 and 1930 had 13 cargo vessels launched at the West Docks. By 1965, Readhead's centenary year, a total of 42 ships had been completed for Strick, the last of these being named *Floristan*. Other shipowners who ordered cargo steamers included Walter Runciman & Company and the Prince Line, both based in Newcastle.

Among the smaller vessels launched by the firm in its first 15 years was the long-serving Tyne paddle tug *President*, completed in 1876. She worked on the river for nearly 70 years, from 1891 until 1959, when she was sold for breaking up. The *President* was one of the four tugs which escorted the great passenger liner *Mauretania* down the Tyne for her delivery voyage in 1907.

However, Readhead's did not rely solely on building contracts for its continued existence. The repair and refitting of ships also became an increasingly important element of the business. Starting with floating repair work, the company went on to open two dry docks, one in 1892 and the other in 1914, which enabled it to expand this side of operations further.

During the First World War, the West Docks constructed 19 cargo ships, three 22-knot 'submarine chaser ' patrol vessels for the Royal Navy, four lighters and converted a cargo vessel into a Royal Fleet Auxiliary ship, RFA *Oletta*.

In common with many other vessels, Readhead-built ships featured in the war casualty lists. The German U-boat campaign took a terrible toll. For example, Hain's tramp steamer *Trevose*, which had been completed in 1896, was torpedoed and sent to the bottom by *U-81* while taking coal from the Tyne to Italy in March 1917. The attack took place in the North Atlantic over 200 miles off Ushant, France. Two men lost their lives, but the rest of the crew were picked up by the Union Castle passenger liner *Alnwick Castle*. Tragically, only hours later it was the turn of the liner to be torpedoed by *U-81* and she too sank. Passengers and crew members boarded lifeboats, but two of the boats disappeared without trace. Three more *Trevose* crew members were among those who died in this second drama.

After the return of peace in November 1918 shipping companies sought replacements for their lost tonnage and this helped to bolster the order books for a short time, but the boom did not last and the 1920s were relatively lean years.

Readhead's Yard at the West Docks, South Shields, on 10 March 1943 at the height of World War II. A cargo ship, vital for the war effort, is taking shape on the stocks. Readhead's and other yards were kept at full stretch during both world wars. Photograph, J.H. Cleet.

Sir James Halder Readhead, a grandson of the founder, took the helm of the company from 1930 and guided it through the difficult years of the early 30s Depression. A popular man who was noted for his kindness, Sir James was known affectionately as 'Little Jimmy'. The company survived the Depression largely because of its shiprepair work. Those two dry docks had proved their worth. Building work was almost non-existent at this time, with only one new ship being completed in the years 1931-1937

During the Second World War Readhead's constructed a total of 35 vessels, including 31 cargo ships, and carried out a great deal of shiprepair work.

The cover of a Readhead's brochure c.1950s, with two cargo ships building. The message on the brochure makes clear that the company was a shiprepairer as well as builder.

The war was not without its dramatic moments for the yard. In April 1941 the West Docks suffered serious damage when it was bombed during a German air raid. A fitting-out shop, the joiners' shop, blacksmiths' shop and saw mills were wrecked. But the yard recovered and stayed in operation to help with Royal Navy as well as merchant vessel work.

Also during the war, the company lost the man who had led it for a decade. 'Little Jimmy' died in 1940, but the Readhead family link with the firm survived after the con-flict. The founder's great grandson, G.H.R. Towers, was chairman of the business in 1967.

The following year the yard was absorbed into the Swan Hunter-led group of shipbuilders, a decade later becoming part of the nationalised British Shipbuilders. The last vessel from the West Docks, the small cargo ship *Singularity*, was launched in 1977. The site then lay unused until closure in 1982. Readhead's had built nearly 600 vessels.

In 1984, the yard was sold off by British Shipbuilders. The dry docks became a private firm, Readheads

Shiprepairers Ltd., continuing the repair work tradition which had been such a major feature of the old company.

The West Docks' shipbuilding berths site was purchased by an old South Shields firm, Captain Frank McNulty Ltd., which concentrated on contracts in the offshore oil platform industry. A 1996 merger with a competitor brought the title Aker-McNulty to the site. This lasted until January 2001 when French firm Technip Coflexip took over.

The yard changed hands again in July 2002, the resulting business taking the earlier name, McNulty Offshore. Marine work thus continues at the site where John Readhead and his hard-working men launched many cargo-carrying princesses of the sea, contributing greatly towards the Tyne's renown as a shipbuilding river.

A memorial plaque to Readhead's workers who died during the First World War and to those who worked for the company during the conflict can be seen on one of the old red-brick buildings fronting the road outside the yard, a reminder of humane values which transcend the world of profit and business.

Ian Wilson, of South Shields, a journalist on the *Evening Chronicle*, remembers being taken to launches at Readhead's as a boy after the Second World War. Ian's father served his time as an apprentice fitter with the company before joining the Merchant Navy and later successfully studying at the South Shields marine school to become an engineering offi-

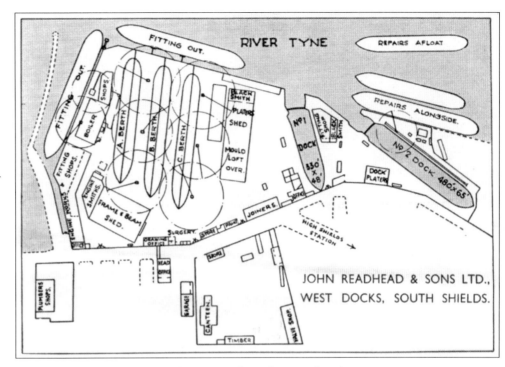

A map showing the West Docks c.1950s, from the same brochure.

cer. Serving an apprenticeship with Readhead's, then going to sea and attending the marine school to gain their 'tickets' was a path taken by a considerable number of South Shields men, a town with a very strong tradition of Merchant Navy seafaring.

Ian writes of a typical launch at the West Docks:

'They were standing around in groups. Dozens of men in double-breasted suits or sports jackets and wearing either a cap or a trilby and with a raincoat over the arm or across the shoulder. It was almost a uniform. They chatted to one another quietly as they stood on the waste ground and the footpath, with an occasional glance towards the dock-yard gate opposite. They were all merchant seafarers, masters and mates and chief engineers and bosuns, ordinary seamen and engine room crewmen; all men with a love of the sea and ships.

'They were standing together that day for one reason only. They wanted to be in at the birth of a ship, a launch at Readhead's yard. Some of them had been for a drink at the nearby pub, the Commercial. Others had strolled from South Shields Market Place about a mile away.

'Once the gates were opened they filed across the road and into the yard in an orderly fashion. Some of the engineers knew the yard well for, like my father, they had served their time as apprentices before going to sea and were quite familiar with ship launches.

'But like me they always found them an exciting occasion. I had been brought up with ships, my first launch being the *Port Auckland*, built for the Port Line by Hawthorn Leslie at Hebburn in 1949, followed shortly afterwards by the *Port Townsville*, beautiful vessels, but sadly broken up now. I was only a child at the time but across the decades the thrill is still with me.

'Readhead's had been building ships for years, mainly for the same customers, Runciman's Moor Line, Hain Steamships and the so-called stan boats (their names always ended with the suffix stan) for Strick. But to these men it didn't matter who the ship was for, what was important was the thrill of see-

Courtesy of South Tyneside MBC

Three vessels in various stages of construction at Readhead's c.1940s. Photograph J.H. Cleet.

ing her go down the ways into the Tyne and then into the arms of the waiting tugs who would shepherd her to the fitting-out quay.

'A ship's bows would tower above you when you first entered the yard. Then your eyes took you down her full length to the stern near the water's edge. She was there in all her glory waiting to be launched.

'The excitement began when the chocks holding her in place were knocked away and the ship began to move. Often there was no official ceremony, no champagne bottle broken across her bows. But this did not matter as the drag chains rattled, the dust rose into the air and the noise reached a crescendo.

'Your brain would become numb, but these merchant seamen would follow the ship down the ways and the faster she went the faster they would run alongside her, but at a safe distance, until her stern kissed the water for the first time. Then the tugs would bustle around to the music of dozens of whistles and sirens blown in celebration by other vessels in the river.

'They were no longer young men and it amazed me where they got the energy from to run in such a way. Perhaps they felt like a father at the birth of a child. It was something that was in the blood passed down from father to son and although on my father's advice I never went to sea, I can understand how they felt. It was an experience never to be forgotten.'

George Coltman, who was born and brought up in South Shields, served his apprenticeship at Readhead's as a joiner from 1942 to 1947. George regards the training he received there as a good one. He recounts how he was in the first batch of apprentices to be given their own toolkits by the company. Previously, all prospective joiners had to supply their own tools.

But it was not as a joinery apprentice that George first started work at the yard. He was initially taken on as a plater's marker boy, but always wanted to become a joiner. Eventually, however, he was given the chance to put his foot on the first rung of the ladder leading to qualification as a craftsman.

He remembers the joiners' shop of 1942 being a new one. It had evidently been rebuilt after that bombing raid in April the previous year. The machinery was also new. But despite the machinery, much of the work was still done by hand. The skills of the craftsman in wood were very much alive. 'Everything was hand-dovetailed and dressed by hand,'

George recalls modestly, but still with the air of a craftsman. He worked on many different jobs, including fitting out ships' cabins and public rooms with furniture. Panelling, handrails and stairways were also among the joiners' tasks.

His hours during this period were 7.30am to 5pm and like so many others who worked in the Tyne shipyards he lived close enough to dash home for his mid-day meal during the dinner hour from 12 noon to 1pm. Sometimes, however, he used the yard canteen, which had been set up during the war and which he describes as 'prefabricated and clean'.

George Coltman, of South Shields, who served his apprenticeship as a joiner at Readhead's, 1942-1947.

Wartime rationing meant that although George and his friends were earning money working long hours, what they could buy with that money was strictly limited. Wartime also brought its incidents. He remembers a bomb narrowly missing a merchant ship being fitted out. Piles of stones and mud were thrown on to her decks by the blast. Luckily, no-one was injured or killed.

Two of the last ships George worked on at the yard, shortly after the end of the war, were the small cargo-passenger steamers *Irish Pine*, completed in 1948, and *Irish Oak* (1949). They were built for Irish Shipping Ltd. He helped to fit out the cabins and public rooms of these vessels, working on hand-veneered panels for wardrobes and on bunks and desks.

Following the end of his apprentice-ship George was paid off because of a slump in orders and went to work in a Sunderland yard. 'I enjoyed working at Readhead's. They gave you a good training and let you get on with the job.'

Today George, and his wife, Nora, live near Readhead Park at Harton, South Shields, the land for which was a gift from the Readhead family. Also nearby is Harton Cemetery, where several members of the Readhead family are buried, including Robert, eldest son of the yard's founder, who died in 1922. Those visiting Robert Readhead's grave, marked by a beautiful stone cross, will learn from the inscription that he was four times mayor of South Shields.

Men at work. Frame-bending at Readhead's Yard, South Shields.

Courtesy of South Tyneside MBC

Bob Koch, also from the town, was employed at the yard as a plater during the 1930s and during the war as a welder. Fascinating details of his working life spring to his mind as he looks back on those far off days.

He remembers that each man received his pay packet in a round tin box, which was re-used every week. Bob also recalls using carbon lamps to light up ships' dark interiors as he worked. Electricity was not provided. And the Strick Line boats stand out in his memory. They provided work when other orders were in short supply. 'We could turn out eight ships a year,' he says, somewhat proudly.

Bob sums up Readhead's in five words: 'They were a friendly firm.'

Little Aberdeen

In June 1853 a boilermaker named Andrew Leslie arrived by steamer at Tyneside's Hebburn Quay. He had made the voyage from his native Scotland and his aim was to set up an iron shipbuilding business on the river. The son of a crofter, Leslie had been brought up in the Shetland Islands, later moving to Aberdeen. While in the Granite City he trained as a boilermaker and also learned ship design and engineering during his spare time. He then operated a small boilermaker's and blacksmith's business in Aberdeen before making the decision to move to the Tyne to become a ship-builder.

Not long after his arrival Andrew Leslie leased land on the banks of the river at Hebburn and set up a shipyard there. Within a few years he was joined by many workmen from Scotland who flocked to the booming yard and earned for Hebburn the nickname 'Little Aberdeen'.

Leslie paid for the building of around 400 houses for the men and their families next to his shipbuilding base. The community responded by making a contribution, both physical and financial, to the building of St Andrew's Church, complete with a 200ft spire, still a prominent feature of Hebburn today. The church, in Ellison Street, cost £10,000. Leslie donated £7,500 of this sum, with the yard men putting in some £1,000 worth of work and the congregation contributing £1,500.

A social centre known as the 'Institute' was built next

St Andrew's Church, Hebburn. Its 200ft spire is a landmark on the banks of the Tyne. Shipbuilder Andrew Leslie helped to pay for the building.

door to the church. The workmen paid for this building via a mortgage and the property was administered by a committee of the men. The Institute featured a large upstairs dance hall running the length of the building and was used for dances and other social functions such as prize-givings. The ground floor was initially used as a school.

The shipbuilder from Aberdeen had wasted little time in constructing his first vessel. This was the auxiliary steam sailing ship *Clarendon*, launched at Hebburn in 1854, only a year after the foundation of the yard. She was 200ft long. During the next 10 years more than 50 ships were launched by Andrew Leslie's company and these included sailing as well as steam vessels.

However, the growth in demand for steamships led to a merger which would strengthen the business. In the 1860s the Newcastle engineering firm of R. & W. Hawthorn, based at the city's Forth Banks, began providing some of the engines for Leslie's vessels. This association continued and in 1886 the two companies merged.

The resulting new company of Hawthorn Leslie now controlled the Hebburn Yard, a marine engine department at St Peter's, Newcastle, and a locomotive-building works at Forth Banks. Each of these sections went on to achieve great success.

Andrew Leslie had retired only a couple of years before this amalgamation. He died peacefully 10 years later in 1894 at his home, Coxlodge Hall, Gosforth. Hundreds of workmen attended the funeral procession from Gosforth to Newcastle Central Station and then a train bore the shipbuilder's coffin northwards to Edinburgh. He was laid to rest in Leith Cemetery, finally returning to his native land. But the shipbuilding base Leslie founded was to live on for many more years.

Between 1860 and the 1890s the Hebburn Yard built over 40 cargo steamers for the shipping line Lamport and Holt, of Liverpool. Foreign customers also came to 'Little Aberdeen'. For example, between 1889 and 1902 the yard created 12 ships for the Russian Volunteer Fleet. These were merchant

Hawthorn Leslie advertises its services in 1925.

R. & W. HAWTHORN, LESLIE & COMPANY, L^{TD}.

S.S. "BADARPUR"
for Burmah Oil Company.

| Shipyard & Dry Dock | Engine Works | Locomotive Works |
| Hebburn-on-Tyne. | St. Peters, Newcastle. | Forth Banks, Newcastle. |

PASSENGER & CARGO VESSELS of all types

RECIPROCATING, TURBINE & DIESEL ENGINES

MAIN LINE & WORKS LOCOMOTIVES of all types

SHIP & ENGINE REPAIRS

passenger steamers capable of serving as auxiliary warships or troopships/stores carriers during emergencies. They included the *Orel, Saratov, Petersburg* and *Kerson*. The last to be delivered, the *Smolensk*, was said to be the largest and fastest in the fleet at that time.

Hawthorn Leslie achieved a good reputation as a warship builder, with torpedo-boat destroyers, forerunners of the modern-day destroyer, becoming a company speciality. Hebburn's first torpedo-boat destroyer, HMS *Sunfish*, was completed in 1895, and between 1897 and 1918 the company received a flood of orders for this type of vessel. Forty-five were completed between 1890 and 1916.

The year 1899 saw the Hebburn Yard launch an epoch-making ship of this class. She was HMS *Viper*, the world's first steam turbine-driven warship. This three-funnel torpedo-boat destroyer achieved what was at that time an astonishing speed of 35 knots on her trials. Her engines were built to the designs of Sir Charles Parsons, Tyneside's brilliant inventor, and supplied by his company. Although the *Viper* was wrecked off the Channel Islands in 1901, she had pioneered the use of turbine engines upon the seas.

Torpedo-boat destroyers were certainly excellent business for the yard, but merchant ships were still launched in considerable numbers. A pioneering ore carrier, the *Sir Ernest Cassel*, was completed at Hebburn in 1910. She had large, spacious holds and electric cranes for speedy unloading of the ore. The vessel was one of the earliest examples of a bulk carrier.

As well as shipbuilding, repair was an important feature of the yard's activity, a dry dock being constructed for this purpose in 1866. Like Readhead's, the company was well

The Russian Volunteer Fleet ship Smolensk, *built by Hawthorn Leslie. She was said to be the largest and fastest in the fleet at the time. Between 1889 and 1902 12 ships were built at Hebburn for this fleet. This photograph appeared in the Mid-Tyne Link of 1905.*

HMS Viper *on trials off the Tyne in 1900. She was the world's first turbine-driven warship.* Viper *was launched at the Hebburn Yard in 1899, but her career was short-lived.*

aware of the importance of the extra income generated by this side of the business.

During the First World War, Hawthorn Leslie was engaged on the construction of 30 ships for the Royal Navy, contributing greatly to the war effort along with other Tyneside yards. The vessels ordered by the Royal Navy were two light cruisers, HMS *Champion* and HMS *Calypso*, and 28 torpedo-boat destroyers, three of these being flotilla leaders. The yard also managed to turn out 12 merchant ships.

The 1920s witnessed the creation of major passenger ships at Hebburn. They included the P&O liners *Ranpura*, launched in 1924, and the *Ranchi*, launched early the following year. Both served on the Tilbury-Bombay run.

A passenger liner was also built for Cunard, the *Andania*, launched in 1921, which served on the Liverpool-Montreal and Southampton-Montreal routes, and other passenger vessels were delivered for the British India Line.

The Hebburn Yard managed to survive the Depression years of the early 1930s, although the workforce was reduced to a low of 600 at one point. But as with other yards on the Tyne, the gathering clouds of war during the mid and late 30s led to a revival in orders. In 1937, 'Little Aberdeen' was the scene for the launching of the 32-knot cruiser HMS *Manchester*.

More warships were to follow, including the famed destroyer HMS *Kelly*, launched in 1939 and captained by Lord Louis Mountbatten. An encounter with the enemy in May 1940 led to the *Kelly* limping back to Hebburn for major repairs and the burial of her dead. The following year she was sunk off Crete.

During the Second World War Hebburn launched 58

The P. & O. passenger liner Ranpura, *which was launched at the Hebburn Yard in 1924. She served on the Tilbury-Bombay run.*

ships, including an aircraft carrier, three cruisers, 16 destroyers, 15 tankers, two fast minelayers and a number of D-Day landing craft. The yard's workforce rose from around 4,000 to more than 6,000.

After the war, Hawthorn Leslie had a share of the orders to replace vessels lost in the conflict and the late 1940s and early 1950s were busy years for the yard. Nine British tankers were among the ships turned out. These included the Shell-owned tanker *Auricula*, which was the first vessel with main engines burning ordinary boiler oil. She was launched in 1946. Also of note was Shell's *Auris*, of 1947. This tanker had diesel electric engines with the innovation of a gas turbine driving one of her alternators.

The output was varied. As well as tankers, it included the *Cortona*, a refrigerated cargo ship completed in 1947 for a Donaldson Line service to South America, the *Salaga* (1947), a cargo vessel for Elder Dempster Line's West Africa run, and the Portuguese passenger liner *Angola* (1948), built for service from Lisbon to Portuguese West and East Africa. Between 1946 and 1950 three cargo passenger ships were completed for the Port Line, which ran services to Australia and New Zealand.

Amongst all this post-war activity the yard still found time to produce the little Mid-Tyne Ferry *No 3*, built in 1949. Driven by diesel engine, she joined the cross-river service from Hebburn to Wallsend and Walker. This busy route was used by many workers travelling to and from their jobs in the days when few people owned cars.

In 1966 Hawthorn Leslie launched a liquefied gas carrier, the *Clerk Maxwell*, for the Ocean Gas Transport Company. The ship was a pioneer. She was able to carry propane, butane or other gases in insulated tanks at sub-zero temperatures.

Other vessels which went down the Hebburn slipways during the 60s included the Royal Fleet Auxiliary tankers *Olwen*, delivered in 1965, and *Olna*, delivered the following year. Next came three more RFA vessels, the landing ships *Sir Tristram* (completed 1967), *Sir Bedivere* (1967), and *Sir Percivale* (1968).

The year 1968 also saw the company merge with Swan Hunter to become part of a new group of Tyneside shipbuilders. In 1977 came another change when the yard was, along with the others, absorbed into the nationalised British Shipbuilders group. Hebburn continued to build vessels, but closed in 1982 after a proud history in which its workforce had produced over 700 ships. Its last vessel was the nuclear fuel carrier *Pacific Swan*, launched in 1978.

By 1985 the site was being used as a shipbuilding training centre and later South Tyneside Council launched plans to turn the yard into a historic Tyne shipbuilding exhibition venue. Sadly, these plans did not come to fruition.

The location of the yard was immediately to the east of Ellison Street, Hebburn. Its dry

The Shell-owned tanker Auricula *is launched at Hawthorn Leslie's yard in 1946.*

dock, slipways and some of the fabrication sheds were acquired by shiprepairers A. & P. Tyne who now occupy this area. The yard's main buildings fronting on to Ellison Street, featuring an arched entrance way, are the premises of a steel fabrication business known as Hawthorn Leslie Fabrications. Homes have also been built on part of the land.

The adjoining riverside area to the east is the site of the former Palmers' Hebburn Yard, which was later used by Cammell Laird and has now been acquired by A. & P. Tyne.

The old shipbuilding company of Hawthorn Leslie is gone, but the way of life in the yard founded by a crofter's son lives on in the memories of its former workmen.

A Speck of Steel

Ron French, a co-author of this book, was born and brought up in Hebburn, almost within the shadow of shipyard cranes. He served an apprenticeship as a marine turner and fitter at the Hawthorn Leslie Yard from 1948 to 1953.

The first ship he worked on was the Shell tanker *Labiosa*, which was specially adapted to carry asphalt. He joined the fitting squad engaged in assembling the pipeline and valve formations for the vessel's pump-room.

Ron writes: 'At this time welding was creeping into British shipbuilding techniques, having been brought to the fore during the recent war by American yards. This half-way stage involved riveting shell plates to frames as ever, but the plate edges were now chamfered and then butt-welded, thus saving on large plating overlaps required for the riveting process. By the early 1950s the yard had fabrication sheds and the first automatic welding machines, producing ever-larger ship sections, built under cover.'

Shipyards were, of course, notoriously dangerous places to work. Ron was lucky never to be seriously injured, but on one occasion he did end up in hospital:

'I can vividly remember getting a steel speck in my eye while operating a grinder and the safety officer/ambulanceman inspecting it and declaring he could not extract the speck with his magnet. So it was suggested that I make my way to the Eye Hospital in Newcastle for treatment and I was supplied with a large wad of cotton wool to hold over the injured eye plus a pass-out note for the gateman.

'Thus it was under my own steam and expense, first climbing the steep bank up to the main bus route and then on my way via a Northern bus from Hebburn to the city, that

Ron French

Co-author of this book, Ron French, by the Tyne. Ron served an apprenticeship as a marine turner and fitter at the Hawthorn Leslie Yard 1948-1953. The St Peter's Marine Engine Works can be seen in the background, left.

I ended up lying on a pristine white-sheeted table.'

After treatment to remove the steel speck, he returned to the yard as quickly as possible. 'The dash back to work was to be there at knocking-off time and collect my time card from the storekeeper and hand it in at the Time Office on the way out, so proving that I had actually been into work that day.'

A major hazard of working in the yards, which was not appreciated at the time, was the danger posed by asbestos. This material, which is now known to be highly damaging to health, provided insulation aboard ships. It was used to cover such items as boilers, steam pipes and engine casings. Even if a man did not handle asbestos he would nevertheless be exposed to its dust. 'There were never any masks provided or warnings given,' says Ron. 'The danger was not realised by anyone. You could see the dust in the air.'

Of ship launchings, he writes: 'Launch days were always a special time and there was a buzz when the managing director was espied leading the lady sponsor through the yard on their way to the launch platform.

'The build-up to a launch involved the shipwrights skilfully removing all the blocks until the vessel sat on her well-tallowed launching ways, held only by wedges at key points underneath, which in turn were held by triggers.

'The oft-recorded time arrived when the lady sponsor broke the bottle, then pulled a symbolic handle or pressed a button. But the real action was almost unobserved beneath the hull. Here the top shipwrights watched for the electronic triggers to be knocked off their holding positions and for gravity to take over.

'The back-up system 40 years ago was a fitter crouched in

*Ken Smith*

An old entrance to the Hawthorn Leslie Yard in Ellison Street, Hebburn. This building is now used by a steel fabrications firm.

a "foxhole" who was obliged in a mis-fire to apply the solution of a 2.5 lb hammer to release the triggers. After that, the forces of gravity and the slope on the berth did the trick.'

Shipyards were strongholds of demarcation between crafts and trades. Ron comments: 'It was truly a serious business. Older tradesmen were very conscious of their links with both the recent and far distant past and were wary of poaching by other trades. Those links went back to the ancient mysteries and guilds of craftsmen who had fought their corner for a share of the work in times gone by.

'What is not perhaps appreciated is that demarcation was ever-present all year round and understood and applied on a day-to-day basis in the yard. For instance, pipework was divided between fitters and plumbers, but amicably so to those in the know. The dividing line was usually accepted by all. The same applied to lathework, where metal turners and brass finishers knew their limits and rarely clashed.'

Ron remembers that the backbone of the yard were the experienced craftsmen in every trade known as 'royals'. Many had given long service to Hawthorn Leslie and were rarely laid off when work was short.

The dry-dock repairs side of the yard's work paid better than the construction side. Those in the repair squad received what was known as a 'dry-dock allowance' which boosted their wages to time-and-a-quarter. In contrast, workmen engaged on the building of ships were on straight 'time' rates, although their wages were occasionally increased by a 'double-bottom allowance' when they worked in confined spaces aboard ships.

The yard did, of course, employ casual workers as well. Many were non-tradesmen. However, the workforce was enlarged temporarily by skilled men such as painters, french polishers, interior joiners and carpet layers when a ship such as a passenger liner was fitting out.

Ron also tells of clocking into work in the morning: 'Virtually every shipyard lies at the bottom of a bank of some sort. Ours had a beauty to hurtle down on foot or bike, en route to make it into work by 7.30am. Timekeeping was always an issue and the memory of the crush to squeeze in past the large fortress-like gates before the gatemen closed them on the dying notes of the buzzer stays with you a long time after.

'The gates remained closed for only a short time, about seven to ten minutes, and then they re-opened to allow the frustrated stragglers in. These men were presented with their time-cards punched with a hole to indicate a pay loss of 15 minutes.'

It was called 'losing a quarter', but the late-comers still managed to reach their muster point in time to join the squad on the trek to their allotted spot in the yard.

Ron French comes from a Tyneside family with shipbuilding and seafaring links going back many years. Maritime influences include his father, born on the Lawe Top at South Shields, who was an Armstrong Whitworth apprentice marine fitter at Elswick and the Walker Naval Yard from 1918 to 1923; a grandfather serving as carpenter with the Tyne-based shipping company Prince Line from 1895 to 1925; an uncle who was a Royal Navy stoker at Jutland; and ancestors who were sea captains on collier brigs sailing out of Shields in the early 19th century.

After finishing his apprenticeship with Hawthorn Leslie in 1953, Ron joined the Merchant Navy in which he served for 28 years as an engineer. He asks, nostalgically: 'How many are left who have vivid memories of the sound of that busy river-life, when shipyard buzzers marked the working day, and even the clatter of rivetting hammers, caulking chisels and ships' sirens were enjoyed, however subconsciously, as evidence of our involvement in the great scheme of things?'

A Gateway to the Oceans

Armstrong's famed Elswick Yard in the West End of Newcastle was among the furthest of the river's yards from the sea, being situated about 11 miles up river from the Tyne piers.

The yard began production in 1884-85 as part of Sir William Armstrong's great Elswick Works and its first ship was the Austro-Hungarian torpedo cruiser *Panther*, launched in 1885.

The opening of this up-river shipbuilding base had been made possible by the completion of the Swing Bridge between Newcastle and Gateshead in 1876, a replacement for an 18th century bridge of low arches which had prevented larger vessels from passing up and down river. Ships could now be launched at Elswick and would reach the sea by passing through the open Swing Bridge, a gateway to the oceans of the world.

In 1882 the Armstrong business, which included the manufacture of guns and hydraulic equipment, had merged with Charles Mitchell's shipbuilding company which operated a yard at Low Walker. The resulting new company was known as Armstrong Mitchell. The two partners

agreed that the Elswick yard would concentrate on building warships while the Low Walker site would specialise mainly in merchant vessels.

Elswick did indeed go on to launch many warships, particularly cruisers, with vessels being delivered to the navies of many countries, including Britain, Japan, China, Argentina,

Guests assemble for the launch of the Austro-Hungarian torpedo cruiser Panther *at the Elswick Yard in 1885. She was the yard's first ship.*

Chile, Brazil, Norway, Portugal, Spain, Italy, Turkey and Romania.

One of the Elswick yard's most important customers was the Imperial Japanese Navy which between 1893 and 1906 took delivery of nine warships from the yard. They included the cruisers *Asama*, *Iwate*, *Idzumo*, *Tokiwa* and *Yoshino*, and the battleships *Hatsuse*, *Yashima* and *Kashima*. Cruisers delivered by the yard fought at the Battle of Tsushima in 1905 in which the Japanese defeated the Russian fleet.

Tyne shipping historian Dick Keys has extensively researched the history of the yard's vessels and has spotlighted a colourful era with the crews of the foreign navies visiting Newcastle to collect their new ships.

Dick tells of the Argentine cruiser *25 de Mayo* (*Veinticinco de Mayo*), the first of five vessels to be built for the Argentine Navy at Elswick. The vessel's designer was Phillip Watts, a brilliant naval architect responsible for a large number of the yard's ships.

The *25 de Mayo* was named after a memorable day in her country's history, 25 May, 1910, when Argentine nationalists unseated the Spanish viceroy at La Plata and so helped to start a trend which ultimately brought down the Spanish South American empire.

The ship was launched on 5 May, 1890, but her completion was delayed by a joiners' strike. When she eventually did emerge from the Tyne her performance was very impressive. During trials in November 1890 she achieved a top speed of 22.47 knots. The *Newcastle Daily Leader* proclaimed that 'speeds realised on these trials have never before been reached by any ship previously built'. On January 29 1891 the *25 de Mayo* undertook gunnery trials off the Tyne. A number of foreign guests were invited to witness these, including representatives of the USA, Russia and Turkey.

Dick writes: 'While completion of the *25 de Mayo* had been slow, instalment payments for her from the Argentine government were equally slow in coming to Armstrong Mitchell. She was still at Elswick at the end of April 1891. Her crew had arrived and her commander-designate, Captain Ramirez, asked that they might be allowed to sleep on board. Permission to do this was reluctantly granted for it was normally a strict company rule not to allow this. It was made clear that the ship remained the property of the company and should not hoist the Argentine flag or leave the river.

'In May the *25 de Mayo* was still held up in the Tyne – but this time moored off Jarrow, awaiting payment of the final instalment.' Eventually, all was settled and in August the fine new cruiser sailed for Argentina, calling at Rio de Janeiro on the way.

Perhaps the most unusually named of the Elswick cruisers was the *O'Higgins*, completed for Chile in 1898. She was named after Bernardo O'Higgins, a Chilean patriot of Irish descent who led his country to freedom from Spanish rule. The ship is sometimes referred to as the *Almirante O'Higgins* or *General O'Higgins*.

The cruiser was launched on May 18, 1897, by Dona Mercedes Valdes de Barros Luco, wife of the Chilean minister in London. The event was watched by naval officers from several nations with ships under construction at Elswick. They included captains from Japan, Brazil, Portugal and China. The *O'Higgins* was fitted with three immensely tall funnels, placed close together slightly forward of amidships, which gave her a distinctive appearance.

The launch of the cruiser O'Higgins *at the Elswick Yard in 1897. She was built for the Chilean Navy and was named after a famous Chilean patriot of Irish descent. The event was watched by naval officers from several nations, including Japan, Brazil, Portugal and China. Dunston Staiths can be seen in the distance.*

During the same year in which this cruiser was launched the Armstrong business underwent a further transformation when it amalgamated with the Manchester-based firm of Sir Joseph Whitworth to become Armstrong Whitworth.

The change did not affect warship building at Elswick which continued unabated into the 20th century. In 1903 the yard launched the Turkish cruiser *Abdul Hamid*. She was renamed *Hamidieh* in 1908 and went on to have a long life. Designed by another of the yard's accomplished naval architects, Josiah Perrett, the *Hamidieh* sank at least three ships during her career. She was in action against the Greeks, Serbians and Bulgarians in 1912-13 and was damaged by a torpedo. In the opening stages of the First World War the *Hamidieh* bombarded the Black Sea coast of Russia. Turkey's long-lived cruiser did not go to the breaker's yard until the 1960s.

Among the many other vessels from the yard were two torpedo gunboats for the Royal Indian Marine. They were the *Plassy* and *Assaye*. The *Plassy* was launched in 1890 and her sister ship the following year. Both vessels were to be stationed at Bombay. Craft were also produced for another corner of Britain's far-flung empire – three small cruisers and two torpedo gunboats were built for the Royal Navy's

The Elswick-built Turkish cruiser Abdul Hamid, *launched in 1903. She is seen here on trials.*

Australian station and received Aborigine names.

It seems that life at Elswick was not all work. Sometimes there were sporting moments. Dick writes: 'In August 1890 the uncompleted *Plassy* was used by the shipyard manager and some selected guests as a viewing platform for the Elswick Works Regatta. The main event was a race from a point below the suspension bridge at Scotswood to a position abreast of the Elswick Works.

'The boats were manned by company workmen and the crews of naval ships completing at the yard. Five oared whalers belonging to the warships were used. In the preliminary round the workmen put up an exceedingly creditable performance by beating the picked crews of the Australian cruisers *Mildura* and *Katoomba*. The combination crew of two other Australian ships, the torpedo gunboats *Boomerang* and *Karrakatta*, were the only warship men to escape defeat.'

During the First World War, Elswick-built warships played their role in the unfolding conflict, two with tragic consequences.

The first of these was the battle-cruiser HMS *Invincible*, which had been launched in 1907 and which with her sister, HMS *Inflexible*, sank the German armoured cruisers *Scharnhorst* and *Gneisenau* at the Battle of the Falklands in December 1914. But the *Invincible* was to meet disaster at the Battle of Jutland on May 31 1916 when she was sunk by German warships with the loss of 1,020 lives. Only six survived. These lucky men were picked up by a British destroyer.

Equally ill-fated was the Elswick-built cruiser HMS *Hampshire*, which had been completed in 1905. She took part at Jutland but was lost only a few days after the battle.

The Brazilian battleship Rio de Janeiro *alongside the fitting out quay at Elswick, launched in 1913. She became the British battleship HMS* Agincourt *and fought at Jutland.*

On June 5 1916 the 22-knot *Hampshire* left Scapa Flow in the Orkneys during a strong gale. She was carrying Lord Kitchener on a wartime mission to Russia. But on the evening of the same day the cruiser struck a mine in heavy seas and sank in a short space of time. Kitchener, his staff and most of the ship's crew lost their lives. The mine had been laid by a U-boat.

The two largest warships to fight with the British fleet at Jutland were also launched at the Elswick Yard. They were the battleships HMS *Agincourt* and HMS *Canada*. Both had originally been ordered by South American navies, but

Britain took them over for service during the First World War.

Agincourt was launched under the name *Rio de Janeiro* for Brazil in 1913 and was equipped with no less than 14 12-inch guns in seven turrets. However, Brazil had financial problems and was unable to pay for this vast battleship. She was therefore sold to Turkey and renamed the *Sultan Osman I*.

Meanwhile, the vessel was moved down river from Elswick to Walker for fitting out. Every effort was being made to deliver her on time for the Turkish Navy. Men worked on the ship at Walker throughout the Newcastle Race Week holidays in the early summer of 1914.

Several weeks afterwards came a dramatic development. The yard workmen must have been surprised when British soldiers boarded the vessel shortly before the outbreak of the First World War in August 1914. She was taken over for service with the Royal Navy.

Turkey seems to have missed sailing out of the river with its 22-knot battleship by a whisker. A Turkish captain and crew had arrived in the Tyne to man the *Sultan Osman I*, but when they attempted to board the vessel they found her guarded by the soldiers. The sailors had no choice but to

The launch of the Chilean battleship Almirante Latorre *at the Elswick Yard in 1913. She became the British battleship HMS* Canada. *The ship was sold back to Chile after the First World War and regained her original name.*

return home on another ship. Britain renamed its newly-acquired 'giant' HMS *Agincourt* and transferred her to the Grand Fleet at Scapa Flow. She survived the war.

Chile had also ordered a battleship from Elswick. Originally named the *Almirante Latorre*, she was launched in 1913 and carried ten 14-inch guns. However, the outbreak of the First World War brought a halt to work on the vessel and she was taken over by Britain in September 1914. Britain then agreed to buy her from Chile and work was re-started. Completed in late 1915, the ship was renamed HMS *Canada*.

Surviving the conflict, the 23-knot vessel was re-purchased by Chile in 1920, who gave her back the name *Almirante Latorre*. Serving many years in the Chilean Navy, the former *Canada* was the longest surviving battleship which had fought at Jutland. She went to the breaker's yard in 1959.

Although the Elswick Yard's output consisted overwhelmingly of warships, it did launch a few merchant vessels. These included four oil tankers, a passenger cargo steamer, a cargo steamer and a cableship.

The yard's last vessel was the aircraft carrier HMS *Eagle*, launched in 1918. She was moved down river to the new Walker Naval Yard for fitting out.

Today, the Elswick Yard has vanished, its site occupied by Newcastle Business Park. It was situated immediately to the west of Water Street, Elswick, and to the south of Scotswood Road. A riverside footpath passes over the site of the building berths in the vicinity of the aptly-named Monarch Road (after a battleship), Hampshire Court and Invincible Drive.

Armstrong Whitworth's Low Walker Yard, which had been founded by Aberdeen-born Charles Mitchell in 1852-53, also made a noteworthy contribution to the river's shipbuilding reputation. Despite the yard's amalgamation with Armstrong it was always known as 'Mitchell's'.

Its output included icebreakers for Russia and the pioneering oil tanker *Gluckauf*, completed in 1886, the prototype of the modern day tanker. Mitchell's went on to produce more than 120 tankers.

The Low Walker yard built over 90 vessels of various types for Russia and Charles Mitchell, together with his business partner Henry F. Swan, set up a shipbuilding yard for the Tsarist government at St Petersburg. Several warships were built there under the company's direction.

In recognition of his services, Tsar Alexander II made Charles a Cavalier of the Order of St Stanislaus, a rare honour for a British shipbuilder.

The list of Russian icebreakers from this yard included the *Yermak* (sometimes spelt *Ermack*), of 1899, the *Sviatogor* and the *Saint Alexander Nevski*, both completed in 1917. The building of these last two ships was supervised by Russian naval architect Yevgeny Zamyatin, who lived for over a year in Jesmond, Newcastle, and later became a distinguished author, best known for his anti-utopian novel *We*, which is considered to have been a significant influence on George Orwell's *1984*.

The characters in *We* live in an authoritarian state where life is ordered with mechanical precision and freedom is sacrificed to an ostensible happiness. People are known by numbers instead of names. Alan Myers, an author and Russian translator who has researched the life and works of Zamyatin, believes the numbers of the characters are taken from the specifications of the

Yevgeny Zamyatin, Russian naval architect and novelist.

Saint Alexander Nevski, Zamyatin's favourite icebreaker.

The hero of the book, D-503, is the designer of a spaceship called the *Integral.* Alan writes that 'his *Integral* has ward rooms, decks and even gunwales, and its shape is the beautiful elongated ellipse of the icebreaker, something about which Zamyatin was prone to rhapsodise'. Alan also comments: 'When the test flight of the spaceship is in preparation, Zamyatin suddenly and for no reason introduces a river and cranes; the whole atmosphere is of a ship launch on the Tyne.'

The location of Mitchell's Low Walker yard was off White Street, opposite its junction with Mitchell Street and a handsome office block built for Armstrong Whitworth in 1915, which is now the Wincomblee Workshops.

The Armstrong Whitworth icebreaker Sviatogor, *built at the company's Low Walker Yard, which had been founded by Charles Mitchell. The name means 'holy mountain'.*

Running parallel with Mitchell Street and alongside the workshops is the old, sunken trackway which led down to the yard. It passes underneath White Street via a tunnel, sloping towards the river.

The trackway begins in the vicinity of the Wincomblee Hotel, but at the time of writing is overgrown and its entrance fenced off. A wall runs alongside one side of the track and the Wincomblee Workshops flank the other side.

Workmen would stream down this underpass route every morning into the yard. Many would have arrived by train at the nearby Walker Station on the Riverside Branch railway. The yard gatehouse was situated next to the trackway entrance and close to the hotel.

Like so many of the Tyne's shipbuilding bases, virtually all of Mitchell's yard has disappeared beneath modern business developments.

Looking at the disused trackway into the yard today, it is

The frames of the Russian icebreaking train ferry Baikal *take shape at Armstrong Mitchell's Low Walker Yard, Newcastle, in c.1895-96. The ship was intended for service on Lake Baikal in the middle of Siberia. The* Baikal *was assembled on the slipway, but was then dismantled. The various sections and parts were afterwards shipped to St Petersburg and then transported thousands of miles to the shores of the lake where the vessel was reconstructed and launched in 1899. A team of engineers from the Tyne led the work of rebuilding the vessel.*

intriguing to think the writer Zamyatin, who drove a Renault motor car, would have used this route on his way to inspect his beloved icebreakers. His car may well have become a familiar site to yard workers. The Renault may also have been familiar to workers at the Wallsend and Neptune yards, for during his stay on Tyneside the Russian novelist also supervised the construction of several small icebreakers built by Swan Hunter & Wigham Richardson.

By the time of Zamyatin's return to Russia in September 1917 the Tsarist government which had sent him on his mission to the Tyne had been overthrown.

And what became of his Low Walker icebreakers? The *Sviatogor* was delivered to the port of Archangel in northern Russia, but the outbreak of the October Revolution altered her career. The Bolsheviks scuttled the ship in 1918 as they tried to block the port to British forces intervening in the north of the country against the revolution.

However, the British raised the *Sviatogor* and incorporated her into the Royal Navy for a few years. When the United Kingdom granted recognition to the Soviet Union she was returned to Russia in late 1921. The year 1927 saw her renamed the *Krasin*, after a People's Commissar for Foreign Trade.

The *Saint Alexander Nevski* was the last of the two ships to be completed and was then seized by the British for service

The Elswick-built Japanese cruiser Asama *off North Shields as she passes down the Tyne in 1899. Elswick supplied many warships to Japan.*

in the Royal Navy, being renamed HMS *Alexander*. She took part in the British intervention in northern Russia and at one point even confronted the *Sviatogor*. However, HMS *Alexander* was left behind in Russia when British forces withdrew in 1919. She was renamed the *Lenin*. Zamyatin's favourite icebreaker had at last been delivered to her intended people.

The Hammerhead Crane

Armstrong Whitworth's Walker Naval Yard in the East End of Newcastle was one of the largest shipbuilding centres on the Tyne and its berths were the venue for the launch of some of the river's most prestigious vessels over a period of more than 60 years.

The yard was constructed as a replacement for the company's Elswick shipbuilding base in the city's West End. Armstrong Whitworth had realised the increasing size of new warships meant that sooner or later they would be unable to pass down river through the Swing Bridge channel to the sea.

Construction of the new Naval Yard at High Walker began around 1910-11 and the facility opened for production in 1913. Extensive river dredging was carried out as part of the scheme. Situated on a long bend in the river, the building berths varied in length, ranging up to around 1,000ft. The fitting out quay was over 2,000ft long.

The site was equipped with powerful cranes, among them a superb 'hammerhead' (cantilever) type, capable of lifting up to 250 tons and situated on the fitting-out quay. This fixed-position crane was to prove its worth in lifting heavy guns and turrets aboard battleships. It was even capable in some instances of reaching across 'double banked' ships moored at the quay. A much smaller crane was fitted on top of the hammerhead crane's gib for lifting light weights when use of the main machinery would have been uneconomic. The building berths were served by large, mobile cranes on rails which could traverse the length of ships under construction. It seems that ten building berths were initially laid out, but this number was later reduced and for much of the yard's life the site featured seven.

The first vessel launched at this major hub of the shipbuilding industry was the *Queen Elizabeth* Class battleship HMS *Malaya*. Her keel was laid down in October 1913 and when completed in early 1916 she was clearly one of the most advanced warships in the British fleet. The *Malaya* was equipped with giant 15-inch guns and featured armour up to a maximum of 13 inches thickness amidships and on turret tops.

The battleship HMS Malaya, *first ship from the Walker Naval Yard.*

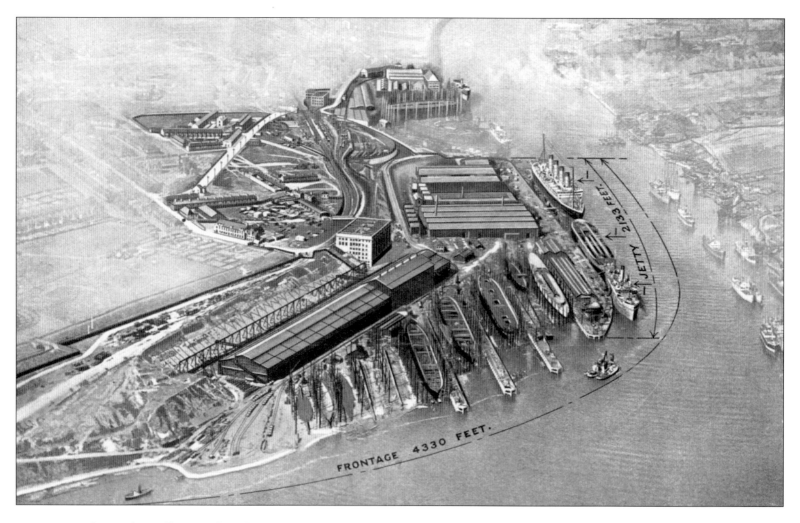

Armstrong Whitworth's Walker Naval Yard, Newcastle, which opened in 1913. Extensive river dredging was carried out as part of the scheme. The building berths varied in length up to around 1,000 feet and the fitting out quay was over 2,000 feet long.

Walker's first battleship was delivered in time to take part in the Battle of Jutland in 1916. Although damaged in the action with the loss of 63 lives, the *Malaya* survived this immense clash between the British and German fleets and went on to serve her country during the Second World War. The ship again proved a survivor and was not broken up until 1948.

In addition to this mighty vessel, the yard's First World War output included the pioneering aircraft carrier HMS *Furious*, whose Sopwith Camel aircraft carried out a raid on German Zeppelin hangars in 1918.

The *Furious* was originally designed as a specialised cruiser with huge 18-inch bombardment guns intended for an invasion of Germany via the Baltic. However, the Baltic campaign was cancelled and on completion the *Furious* emerged from the Tyne in 1917 with a flying-off deck and hangar fitted forward of the bridge.

Later, her superstructure was removed to convert he into a fully-fledged early-style aircraft carrier with a landing-on deck stretching most of the length of the ship and a short flying-off deck at a lower level forward. This lack of a superstructure earned the *Furious* the nickname 'The Flat Iron.' She survived the Second World War, by which time she had

The Cunard passenger liner Ausonia, *completed at the Walker Naval Yard in 1921 for the company's Canadian services.*

been given back a visible funnel and an island superstructure situated on the extreme starboard side of the ship.

Another cruiser intended for the Baltic campaign was HMS *Courageous*. She was launched at the Walker Naval Yard in 1916 and during the 1920s was also converted into an aircraft carrier.

Additional vessels from Walker during the First World

War included the light cruisers HMS *Danae*, HMS *Centaur* and HMS *Concord*. Work also proceeded on a number of submarines both at Elswick and Walker. The year 1919 saw the delivery of two more light cruisers, HMS *Dunedin* and HMS *Delhi*.

In the period between the two world wars the Walker Naval Yard turned to merchant shipbuilding as well as naval. Several important passenger ships were constructed. They included the two-funnel Swedish liner *Gripsholm*, which after her completion in 1925 became the first transatlantic ship to be driven by diesel motor engines. During the Second World War the *Gripsholm* served as an International Red Cross ship.

The yard also launched two A-class passenger liners for Cunard's Canadian services. These were the *Ausonia*, completed in 1921, and the *Ascania*, completed in 1925. Both served mainly on the London-Montreal run and survived the Second World War. The conflict led to *Ascania* doing spells of duty as an armed merchant cruiser and as a troopship, while *Ausonia* also served as an armed cruiser and later a repair vessel.

The Swedish passenger liner Gripsholm, *completed at the Walker Naval Yard in 1925. She was the first transatlantic liner to be driven by diesel motor engines. Photograph by Parry.*

In 1923 the workforce completed the P&O passenger liner *Mongolia*, which operated on the Britain-India-Australia run during her early years. The *Mongolia* went on to have a varied career lasting over 40 years.

Two important jobs were carried out by the yard soon after the First World War. In 1919-20 the huge Cunard liner *Aquitania* was converted from a coal-burning ship to an oil-

A view of the Walker Naval Yard from Bill Quay, 1919-20. The four funnels of the Aquitania *can be seen at the fitting out quay with numerous ships moored in the river.*

The magnificent Cunard passenger liner Aquitania *leaves the Walker Naval Yard 26 June 1920 after being reconditioned and converted to oil burning from coal.*

firing one at Walker, and in 1921-22 it was the turn of another giant Cunard passenger ship, the *Berengaria*, to receive the same treatment. Both ships were given major refits at the same time. These huge liners dominated the riverside scene in the Walker area for months and were an impressive sight from the opposite bank of the Tyne at Hebburn and Bill Quay.

At the end of 1927 many of Armstrong Whitworth's business interests, including the Naval Yard, were merged with those of Vickers to form Vickers-Armstrongs Ltd. But this amalgamation of two large companies did not prevent the yard from closing in 1928 because the order book had dried up. Unemployment was rising.

The yard did not open again until 1930 when work began on the construction of the Furness Withy passenger liner *Monarch of Bermuda*. This impressive-looking three-funnel ship was built for the New York-Bermuda cruise service. The contract provided much needed work during the Depression, although after the delivery of this ship in November 1931 the yard closed again until late 1934.

The *Monarch of Bermuda* had an eventful career. She rescued 71 people from the fire-engulfed American liner *Morro Castle* in 1934 and served as a British troopship during the Second World War. The liner carried soldiers to the Norwegian, Italian and North Africa campaigns. After the war, the ship was badly damaged by a fire while undergoing a refit at Hebburn in 1947. She was, however, eventually repaired and reconstructed, becoming an emigrant ship taking Britons to Australia during the early and mid 1950s. She had been renamed the *New Australia*.

Among the Royal Navy orders which came to Walker between the world wars was the battleship HMS *Nelson*. Featuring colossal 16-inch guns and a tall control tower which dwarfed her funnel, the *Nelson* left the Tyne for delivery in 1927. A strange-looking vessel, she was perhaps one of the least beautiful ships launched on the river, but she nevertheless survived the Second World War.

As we have seen, the Depression of the early 1930s saw Walker hit hard, in common with other yards on the river. Empty building berths and unemployment became the norm. However, the order books revived during the mid and late 30s as war became increasingly likely. The spectre of conflict led to another giant fighting vessel being delivered from the Walker Naval Yard, the battleship *HMS King George V*. Launched into the Tyne appropriately by the late monarch's son, King George VI, in February 1939, the ceremony was watched by around 20,000 people.

The ship, which carried ten 14-inch guns with a range of 21 miles, was completed in late 1940. Her armour was up to 16 inches thick. The *King George V* left the river at night because of the German bombing threat. Under cover of the darkness, Tyne pilot Captain J.Y. Duncan guided the huge vessel towards the North Sea without mishap. By this time, the numbers of men working at the Walker Naval Yard had risen to more than 4,200. The *King George V* went on to play a major role in the sinking of the German battleship *Bismarck* in 1941.

Other Second World War vessels built at this large shipbuilding base included the cruiser HMS *Sheffield* (launched 1936) and the aircraft carrier HMS *Victorious* (launched 1939). They too played a role in the operation against the *Bismarck*. The cruisers HMS *Nigeria* and HMS *Uganda* and 24 destroyers, including HMS *Cossack*, HMS *Mashona*, HMS *Eskimo*, HMS *Hero,* and HMS *Hereward*, were also born at Walker during this period.

During the war, a German aircraft dropped two bombs, one of which narrowly missed Walker's giant hammerhead crane. It was rumoured the aircraft had deliberately targeted the crane with the aim of bringing it crashing down to wreak havoc on the fitting-out quay and possibly block the Tyne.

The raid took place on the morning of January 27 1941 and it is likely it was an opportunist attack by a single plane taking advantage of cloud cover over the North Sea. It is possible, however, that the plane had been damaged and was jettisoning its bombs as it began its escape flight back to Germany. At least one observer noticed that it came in low, flying down the Tyne towards the sea.

The first bomb exploded on the quay, leaving a 25ft diameter crater. The second bomb failed to explode, leaving a hole in the fitting-out quay near the foot of the crane. It was soon defused by the Army. It was reported that 31 workers were injured in the raid, with some of the casualties being treated at the yard first aid post and those more seriously hurt being taken to the Royal Victoria Infirmary, to Walker Hospital and to a first aid post in Wharrier Street, Walker. The windows of the anglesmiths' shop were blown in, showering men inside with glass.

Following the war, the yard's orders included a series of

A brigade of bowlers. Guests at the launch of the large passenger liner Monarch of Bermuda *at the Walker Naval Yard in March 1931.*

stately passenger liners. The *Ocean Monarch,* completed in 1951, was Furness Withy's replacement for the fire-damaged *Monarch of Bermuda.* Smaller than her predecessor, the *Ocean Monarch* had only one funnel but was elegant, stylish and looked not unlike a large royal yacht.

Later, came two prestigious queens for the Canadian Pacific Line. The first of these was the *Empress of England,* launched at the yard in 1956. Her sister, the *Empress of Canada,* entered the Tyne in 1960, the launch ceremony being performed by Mrs Deifenbaker, wife of the Canadian prime minister.

The ship was delivered the following year for the Liverpool-Montreal route, making calls at Greenock and Quebec City. At 27,280 gross registered tons the *Empress of Canada* was the second largest passenger liner built on the river, being exceeded only by Swan Hunter & Wigham Richardson's legendary *Mauretania* of 1907.

Other post-war achievements at Walker included the building of a series of Blue Funnel Line cargo passenger liners, the first being the *Autolycus,* of 1949. Orders from Blue Funnel continued into the 1960s. Oil tankers too featured in the order books during the 50s and 60s, with vessels being delivered to several owners, including Esso and Shell.

The last passenger ship constructed at the Walker Naval

Ron French

The hammerhead crane towers above the newly launched passenger liner Empress of England *at the Walker Naval Yard, 1956.*

Yard was the *Northern Star.* Completed in 1962, she was built for Shaw Savill and Albion Line's round-the-world cruise service, which she operated in partnership with her sister, the *Southern Cross.*

The yard went on to become part of the Swan Hunter-led group of Tyne shipbuilders, eventually being merged into the nationalised British Shipbuilders. Afterwards, it came under Swan Hunter ownership. The final vessel launched at the Walker Naval Yard was the refrigerated container ship *Dunedin,* which entered the water in February 1980. She was

Canadian Pacific's passenger liner Empress of Canada, *which was completed at the* Walker Naval Yard, *Newcastle, in 1961. The vessel is seen here on her trials. At 27,280 gross registered tons, the ship was the second largest passenger liner built on the Tyne, being exceeded in size only by the* Mauretania *of 1907. The* Empress of Canada *was launched at Walker in May 1960 by the wife of the Canadian Prime Minister John Diefenbaker. The ship ran on the Liverpool-Greenock-Quebec City-Montreal route until late 1971. Later she became a full-time cruise liner.*

built for the Shaw Savill & Albion Line.

The modern aircraft carriers HMS *Illustrious* and HMS *Ark Royal* were both fitted out at Walker during the 1980s after being launched at Swan Hunter's Wallsend Yard. *Ark Royal* was the last to depart. She left the river in 1985 and then the fitting out quay at the Naval Yard fell silent. The berths were already empty.

Today, the site is occupied by an industrial estate, the Walker Offshore Technology Park, with several companies operating on the land where great ships once took shape. Some of the roads on or near the site recall the heyday of the Naval Yard – Malaya Drive, Nelson Road and Empress Road. The giant hammerhead crane continues to dominate the riverside and is still used, a survivor of that wartime bomb scare. Another large crane also survives nearby. Few other traces are left of the great shipbuilding complex at Walker, now lost forever.

Co-author Ken Smith at the site of the former Walker Naval Yard, the hammerhead crane in the background.

Coconut Launchings

Alan Mather, of Whitley Bay, was an apprentice joiner at the Walker Naval Yard from 1942 to 1947 and remembers the hammerhead crane well. Two of the first ships he worked on after starting in the yard at the age of 16 were the cruiser HMS *Swiftsure* and the monitor (large gun ship) HMS *Abercrombie*.

'Gun turrets would be floated down river from the Elswick Works on barges and the hammerhead crane would lift them aboard the warships,' said Alan. 'I remember seeing the huge turret lifted into the *Abercrombie*. Her 15-inch guns were said to be from one of the monitors built by Palmers during the First World War.'

His working hours as an apprentice were from 7.30am to 5pm with a dinner break from noon to 1pm. This was a 47-hour week and included Saturday mornings. Overtime, was, of course, often worked during the war. One of his first jobs as an apprentice joiner was making stowage fittings for hammocks aboard a warship and racks for bombs.

Alan travelled every morning from Whitley Bay to Walker, using the Riverside branch railway which had stations at such places as Percy Main, Carville (Wallsend), St Anthony's, Byker and St Peter's. This line was used by large numbers of shipbuilding workers. The station at Walker was close to the yard and Alan joined the huge mass of workmen as they swarmed in through the gates at the start of the long working day. Many, of course, lived near the yard, and walked or cycled to their job.

Following the end of the war in 1945 merchant ship orders began to loom much larger in the yard's order books

Alan Mather

The Ellerman cargo passenger liner City of York *during fitting out at the Walker Naval Yard in 1953. Photographed by Alan Mather from the fire escape outside his office.*

and Alan helped make the furniture for the specialised locomotive-carrying ship *Beljeanne*, which was equipped with massive derricks for lifting the engines on and off.

After completing his apprenticeship, he transferred to the joinery drawing office alongside the fitting-out quay and rose to become assistant foreman in charge of this department.

One of his proudest moments came when he and two other senior men, Jimmy Swan and Tom Rickaby, were given the job of designing the public rooms for four Ellerman Line cargo-passenger ships, the *City of York, City of Exeter, City of Durban* and *City of Port Elizabeth*, all of which were launched at Walker.

Three of the liners had identical interiors. He remembers that half the cabins in each vessel had furniture in bird's eye maple and half in French walnut. 'We found the occasional bullet from the First World War in the walnut.'

Alan was responsible for designing the lounge and veranda café and he recalls Tom worked on the children's nursery and smoke room drawings. The restaurant was a joint effort by all three men. The fourth and last liner to be built, the *City of Durban*, differed from the others in having antique Georgian pine panelling. Alan greatly enjoyed his work on these liners and still recalls the job with a mixture of pride and pleasure.

He also tells of the time in 1960 when the Naval Yard

Alan Mather

An army of foremen enjoy their annual dinner at the Walker Naval Yard, Newcastle, in the early 1950s. Alan Mather (with moustache) is pictured centre foreground. The yard's general manager was among those attending.

launched two warships for the Indian navy, the *Beas* and *Betwa*. 'Coconuts were used instead of bottles of champagne at the launch ceremonies,' says Alan, who with Jimmy Swan was given the job of making sure that the nuts broke and gave forth their milk when they hit the bows of the ships. They carried out various experiments and then decided to use a hacksaw to weaken the shells. The trick worked and the coconuts duly broke when the ceremonies were performed by two Indian ladies.

Alan has a host of happy memories of his days at Walker. For example, he worked on the planning and drawings for the *Empress of Canada* and later received a Canadian Pacific tie as a gift in appreciation of his efforts. In addition, he and other foremen sailed out of the Tyne on the trials of the *Empress of England* and he still has a photograph of them standing on the stern of the ship.

One of his most vivid memories was travelling to work on the train from Whitley Bay and seeing the *Monarch of Bermuda* after she was hit by fire while alongside the quay at Hebburn. 'Her hull plates were buckled and blackened and the bridge also showed the effects of the blaze.'

The last Walker vessel Alan worked on was the passenger liner *Northern Star*, completed in 1962. The Queen Mother launched the ship but had injured her ankle and had to use a wheelchair. He recalls that two brothers, Stan and Norman Bell, of Cullercoats, were given the job of pushing the Queen Mother around the yard in the wheelchair because they were accustomed to doing the same for their own mother. By this time Alan was heavily involved in planning matters. After this, he left Vickers-Armstrongs and went on to hold senior and managerial positions in various companies. However, he regards his 20 years spent at the Walker Naval Yard, during which time he made many friends, as very special.

Fred McCabe, of Walker, Newcastle, was a shipwright at the Naval Yard for 44 years, joining as an apprentice in 1934 at the age of 16. He has lived in Walker all his life and did not have far to go to get to work. Like Alan Mather, his hours were 7.30am to 5pm, with an hour for his mid-day meal, but he remembers that sometimes a half-shift of over-time would be worked, taking the finishing time to 9pm. 'It was a long day,' he says.

In common with many other yard men from the Walker

Fred McCabe

A photograph of Fred McCabe as a boy of 12 which still hangs in his home at Walker. Flanking him are his father, who worked at the Neptune Yard, and his grandfather, who was a seagoing engineer. Ships clearly run in the family.

area, Fred generally went home for dinner, riding on his bicycle, and his wife had his meal ready for him. In his last years at the yard he used the company canteen. 'Almost every yard had a canteen,' he says.

Like Ron French, Fred McCabe recalls 'losing a quarter' when he failed to reach the yard in the mornings before the gates shut. Even though he might be only a few feet or seconds away before they closed, he still had his wages reduced.

Fred's first two ships during his time as an apprentice were the destroyers *Hero* and *Hereward*. He also worked on submarines, small landing craft and the *King George V* as well as many others, including the *Sheffield*.

He recounts the story of the keel of a battleship named HMS *Lion* being laid down and then work on her being halted. The order was cancelled and the vessel never built. Nevertheless, Fred and his workmates were told by the management that if anyone asked about HMS *Lion* they were to reply that she had been completed and had sailed away to sea. It seems to have been an attempt at wartime misinformation with the aim of fooling the enemy.

As a shipwright Fred was involved in the work on a vessel 'from the keel upwards'. His specialities were stems and sterns, putting the sections of the extreme fore and aft ends of ships into place and preparing them for welding or riveting. He also worked in wood, laying out timber decks. He helped lay decks on the *King George V* and carried out caulking to the timbers, which involved sealing the spaces between the planks with oakham and pitch. One of the tools he used during deck work was an adze, an axe-like implement with a curved blade. Adzes had been used by shipwrights for hundreds of years and Fred still has his adze in his tool shed at home, an echo of the distant past. Shipwrights working on the Tyne in the 18th century and earlier would have been familiar with this tool.

Fred recalls the dangers encountered in the shipyard and tells of several accidents. One of the worst in his experience occurred when a gang of men were engaged in putting a steel plate into position on a merchant ship. The block and tackle lifting the section snapped and a man was knocked off the scaffolding and killed.

He remembers another accident in which a man was killed when a funnel being lifted off a railway wagon fell and crushed him. A third man, a fitter, died when a submarine turned over on its side while under construction on a berth. Two other workers lost their arms in separate accidents involving yard trains.

Fred himself narrowly escaped death at the Naval Yard in the early 1950s. Some men were lowering a steel plate, about 3ft long and one inch thick, towards a deck on which he was walking. The plate slipped out of its rope and he was struck on the head. Luckily, it was a glancing blow, but despite this he suffered a major gash wound to his forehead and scalp. He was taken to the Royal Victoria Infirmary, Newcastle, where the wound needed 30 stitches. Fred also received an injury to his nose and broken teeth in the accident. He was off work for two weeks and a scar is visible on his forehead to this day. As was usual in those days, he had not been provided with a safety helmet.

Fred also tells of the asbestos dust which could frequently be seen in the air. The particles were at their most prominent when illuminated by shafts of sunlight.

However, he also has many pleasant recollections of his

life at the yard. He remembers the tall, handsome office block which housed managers, administrative staff, drawing office personnel, the purchasing department, a ship model room and timekeepers. 'It was a shame they pulled it down. It was a marvellous building.'

Other aspects of the yard which stand out in his memory include a very long shed, which was used for fabrication and other work. The shed was situated behind the building berths, of which there were seven during his time there. The shed and other parts of the yard were connected to the berths via railway lines. The yard had three steam locomotives of its own, with names suggestive of strength such as 'Elephant' and 'Lion'. Extensive workshops were located behind the fitting-out quay.

Fred was in the yard when the bomb dropped near the hammerhead crane and says an elderly man working as a cleaner was found dead in the rubble of the crater left behind. 'It's a good job that bomb did not explode. Many more men would have been killed if it had. It was over 5ft long.'

Despite the dangers, he enjoyed his many years at the Naval Yard which he describes with obvious delight as 'the best yard on the river'. Commenting on the four Ellerman liners, he says: 'They were beautiful boats. They were fitted out like hotels. I don't suppose they could produce ships of that quality today.'

Turners, Tyne & Wear Archives

The Shaw Savill passenger liner Northern Star *in dry dock, probably at Hebburn before her hand-over to the owners in 1962.*

Rise and Fall

In April 1852 an iron paddle tug, the *Northumberland,* was launched at the Palmer Brothers' yard in Jarrow, on the southern bank of the Tyne. She was the first vessel from a famed company which would go on to build more than 900 ships over the next 80 years.

Charles Mark Palmer had set up the business with his brother George barely a year earlier on the site of the yard which had been used by Simon Temple Junior to build wooden sailing ships during the early 1800s. Now the scene was set for a new venture in which iron and steel would take centre stage.

Palmers' second ship was the pioneering iron steam collier *John Bowes,* the first vessel to demonstrate conclusively the advantages of carrying coal by steamship and the first iron steamer built specifically for the coal run from the North-East to London.

Over the next 50 years or so the village of Jarrow was to grow into a town of around 40,000 people, a development linked directly to the success of Palmers Yard which was the main source of employment. However, the community's dependency upon one company was to prove a fatal weakness during the Depression years of the early 1930s.

The Jarrow yard was equipped with its own blast furnaces and iron and steel works, the metal produced being used to build Palmers' ships as well as being exported worldwide. Iron ore for this purpose was shipped to the yard's quayside by a fleet of the company's own vessels. Much of the ore came from mines which Charles Palmer had acquired in North Yorkshire.

Boiler and engine works were also established on the site and by 1909 the complex stretched nearly three quarters of a mile along the riverside opposite Howdon.

In addition to a series of early steam colliers, Palmers also launched many oil tankers, the first of these being the *Era,* of 1887.

The building of warships was another important element of the order books, Palmers' creations including the battleships HMS *Russell,* HMS *Lord Nelson* and HMS *Hercules* of the early 1900s. Also launched were two battleships named HMS *Resolution,* one taking to the water in 1892 and the other in 1915. Jarrow's largest warship was the battlecruiser HMS *Queen Mary,* launched in 1912 and tragically sunk at the Battle of Jutland in 1916 with the loss of 1,266 lives.

Smaller vessels produced included a large number of torpedo-boat destroyers, 28 being constructed between 1895 and 1910. Cruisers, particularly in the 1880s, proved to be another important feature of the order books. In all, the company delivered more than 100 ships to the Royal Navy.

In 1859 Palmers acquired the shipyard at Willington Quay which had been operated by the pioneering Coutts before he was forced to give up his business. The site became Palmers' Howdon Yard, its products including steam colliers and tor-

A ship being fitted out alongside Palmers Hebburn Yard c.1910. The yard built mainly merchant ships and featured the largest dry dock on the North-East coast. The dock had originally been installed by the firm of Robert Stephenson.

pedo-boat destroyers.

In 1911-12 the company took over another yard, this time at Hebburn, which had been used by the firm of Robert Stephenson for shipbuilding. The site was a short distance up river from Jarrow and next to Hawthorn Leslie's Hebburn Yard. At about the same time, Palmers gave up their yard at Howdon, which was acquired by shipbuilders J.T. Eltringham.

The First World War brought tragedy to the Jarrow yard when 12 men working night shift were killed in a Zeppelin bombing raid on June 15, 1915. The youngest was aged 18.

The 1920s saw the company engaged on building a series of oil tankers, the largest being the *San Gaspar* and *San Gerardo*, launched for Eagle Oil.

The collapse of Palmers came during the Depression of the early 1930s. Financial weaknesses within the business meant that it was unable to survive the economic storm.

Its last ship, the destroyer HMS *Duchess*, was launched at Jarrow in 1932.

By the beginning of 1933, the year in which the Jarrow Yard closed, more than 7,000 people were unemployed in the town. This was around 70 per cent of Jarrow's entire workforce. The company was heavily in debt.

The distress and poverty caused by the closure led directly to the Jarrow Crusade of 1936. Two hundred unemployed workmen from the town marched over 280 miles from Jarrow to London to urge government action to provide jobs for the community. The plight of the town's people touched many hearts.

By this time, the Jarrow Yard had been sold to National Shipbuilders Security Ltd., a company formed by other ship-building firms to buy up and close down shipyards to reduce 'over-capacity' in the industry. No shipbuilding was to be allowed on the Jarrow site for a period of 40 years. Most of the yard was dismantled, including its distinctive elliptical-shaped cranes, and its equipment sold.

But the firm's Hebburn Yard, which featured the largest dry dock on the North-East coast, survived. It was sold to Vickers-Armstrongs and used for shiprepair under the name Palmers Hebburn Ltd. This repair base proved a valuable facility during the Second World War. A new dry dock was later built to replace the old one.

In 1973 Swan Hunter bought the Palmers Hebburn Yard from Vickers and between 1973 and 1982 seven ships were built in the dock. In the 1990s the yard changed hands again and was operated by the Cammell Laird company which used it for shiprepair and refitting. Cammell Laird also built a vessel in the dock, a small roll-on roll-off ferry for Danish owners. In 2001 the yard was acquired by shiprepairers A. &P. Tyne.

The site of Palmers' Jarrow Yard is today occupied by a modern industrial estate and is situated to the north and north east of Western Road. The Rohm and Haas chemical company is one of the main businesses on the estate. A small section of the yard's eastern boundary wall still stands close to the Tyne foot and cycle tunnel entrance. This is all that survives of Charles Palmer's once mighty empire of ships, iron and steel.

A grand occasion. The Duke and Duchess of York at the launch of the cruiser HMS York *at Palmers Yard, Jarrow, 17 July 1928. The yard closed in 1933, sparking mass unemployment in Jarrow. The cruiser was the last large warship launched by Palmers. Photograph by Parry.*

Not a Single Ship

etal would gradually supersede wood as the predominant shipbuilding material of the 19th century, but timber construction continued for many years at some sites on the Tyne. During this period shipbuilding firms came and went, some lasting only a few years and others operating for a decade or more. One business sometimes succeeded another on the same site and three or more concerns might occupy the same location over a period of many years. An example of a site used by a succession of shipbuilding firms was the yard of William Cunningham at St Lawrence in Newcastle. He set up his business in c.1839 and seems to have preferred the 'old ways' of wooden construction. The yard's output included full-rigged ships, barques, snows and schooners.

Cunningham's largest vessel was probably the full-rigged ship *Kensington*, launched in February 1855. The *Newcastle Daily Journal* reported the event: 'A noble vessel, the *Kensington*, property of Messrs. G. W. Beckwith & Co., of this port, was launched by Mr Cunningham at St Lawrence. A large number of persons assembled to witness the launch and the beauty of the lines of the ship was a subject of general commendation. Miss Emily Beckwith officiated as sponsor and at 3pm the noble ship made a fine run into the Tyne, amid cheering and the firing of guns. She will be completely rigged in this port and then proceed to the Thames to be employed in the Indian and Australian trades. The

Kensington is the largest vessel built within sight of the Newcastle Bridge. A larger vessel for the same owner is on order.' The newspaper added that after the launch the owners invited many of their friends to a meal furnished by a Mr Carmon of the George Inn and set out in Mr Cunningham's yard lofts. 'Toasts and applause followed.' William Cunningham's business lasted until c1860 when he sold out to G.C. Hutchinson. Several other shipbuilding firms were to follow on the same site. By 1900, however, launchings had ceased at this location. The site is now under the eastern extensions of Newcastle Quayside, not far from Spillers Mill.

William Rowe's wooden yard at St Peter's, Newcastle, was taken over by Alderman Thomas Smith, a rope manufacturer, and his sons William and Thomas, in 1810. Following his death, his sons carried on the business. The firm, which became known as T. & W. Smith, continued to launch mainly wooden vessels at the site until the 1860s. From 1828 to 1861 the output at St Peter's included large sailing ships known as East Indiamen, intended, as their name implied, for trade to India and the Far East.

The first of these was the *Duke of Roxburghe* of 1828, and Smith's went on to launch larger and improved ships of this type. They included the *Duke of Northumberland*, launched at St Peter's in 1831, the *Ellenborough* (1842), the *Gloriana* (1843) and the *Hotspur* (1851). The high point came in 1846-48 when they built the *Marlborough* and

LAUNCH OF THE "BLENHEIM," EAST INDIAMAN, 1600 TONS BURTHEN, AT NEWCASTLE-UPON-TYNE.

Crowds at the launch of the East Indiaman Blenheim *in 1848 at T. & W. Smith's St Peter's Yard, Newcastle. The yard launched many fine full-rigged sailing ships for the trade to India. Smith's were eventually to move all their shipbuilding to a yard which they operated at North Shields. The North Shields yard evolved into the Smith's Dock shiprepair complex of the 20th century. Picture from the Illustrated London News.*

Blenheim, the largest and most magnificent. Nearly all these ships were owned and operated by Smith's on the India run.

Their last East Indiamen were the St Peter's-built *St Lawrence* of 1861, and the North Shields-built *Cheviot* (1862) and *Brisbane* (1867).

The St Peter's Yard and an adjacent site, John Rogerson's Yard, were combined in 1863-64 into one business known as the Tyne Iron Shipbuilding Company, sometimes referred to as the St Peter's Iron Shipbuilding Company. This new firm ran fairly successfully until c.1871 when the site was sold to Newcastle engineering company R. & W. Hawthorn who moved their marine engineering department there. As we have seen, Hawthorn's would merge with Andrew Leslie's Hebburn Yard in 1886. The St Peter's site is today occupied by St Peter's Marina and modern housing.

However, T. & W. Smith had already opened another yard, on the Limekiln Shore at North Shields, immediately down river from Coble Dene, building iron vessels there from c.1852-1853 onwards as well as wooden ones. The first iron steamer from the North Shields yard was the *Zingari*, launched in 1854.

The company were no strangers to North Shields for much earlier, in 1814, they had leased a dry dock known as Laing's, which was a little further down river from the Limekiln Shore. Laing's Dock is said to have become too small for their needs and in 1850 they opened a new dock on land adjoining the yard. Ships continued to be built at Smith's North Shields base for many years, although eventually it was decided the site should concentrate mainly on shiprepair. A new business was formed known as the Smith's Dock Company in c1891-92 and a floating pontoon dock was constructed to enable the yard to handle more vessels. Later, a second pontoon was added.

A landmark in the history of the business came in 1899 when Smith's merged with H.S. Edwards & Sons which operated the nearby Bull Ring shiprepair docks. A steam trawler-building yard known as Edwards Brothers situated between the two sites was also absorbed. The name Smith's Dock Company was retained. The result was the formation of a large docks complex at North Shields which was to flourish as a major shiprepair business during the 20th Century, gaining a particularly sound reputation for handling tankers and Royal Fleet Auxiliary vessels.

Small seagoing vessels, including trawlers, continued to be launched at the North Shields yard into the early 1900s. However, in 1910 the company moved all its shipbuilding operations to a new base at South Bank, Middlesbrough, on the Tees. But North Shields remained its most important shiprepair facility. By 1930 Smith's were advertising themselves as the largest shiprepairers and dry dock owners in the world. The North Shields yard was used for repair and refitting well into the 1990s, although under different ownership. Today, the Smith's Dock site is derelict, but the old dry docks themselves are still in place.

H.S. Edwards & Sons, the firm which had amalgamated with Smith's, also had dry docks across the river at South Shields where it had operated an old-established shiprepair business. In earlier years this concern had constructed sailing vessels. The Edwards family business could trace its origins to c1812 when George Straker joined a partnership operating the High Dock at South Shields for shipbuilding and repair. The High Dock had been founded by the Wallis family.

By 1830, Straker's son-in-law, James Edwards, was in charge of the dock. James was succeeded in 1856 by his son, Harry Smith Edwards, who had been a sea captain. The firm concentrated mainly on shiprepair from c.1870 when it began handling iron vessels. The Edwards business later expanded to the Bull Ring land across the river at North Shields where two dry docks were developed before the merger with Smith's.

The old Edwards High Docks at South Shields were for many years part of the Smith's Dock Company empire but from 1924 the site was absorbed into Readhead's yard.

In 1882 Harry Smith Edwards and his sons, together with a business partner, had opened at shipyard on the northern bank at East Howdon, close to the Northumberland Dock. This yard built 75 small vessels and operated until 1898.

T. & W. Smith certainly continued to launch ships of wood until the 1860s, but one of the last major builders in this traditional material on the river were Gaddy & Lamb, of Tyne Main, Gateshead. This firm had been established before 1840 and went on to launch a variety of sailing vessels, including full-rigged ships and barques. Gaddy & Lamb continued building in wood until c. 1875-1880 while the Tyne iron shipbuilding boom went on all around them. Their yard was located on the foreshore below the Ship Inn, close to Gateshead International Stadium.

A little further down river, at Bill Quay, Gateshead, is the site once occupied by Wood Skinner, one of the most prolific smaller shipyards on the south bank of the river. Their vessels were of iron and steel. This firm built more than 330 small and modest-sized ships, including coasters, trawlers, colliers and passenger steamers. During the First World War

A Smith's Dock advertisement from 1930. The oil tanker Mitra *is seen entering the new No. 5 Dock at North Shields.*

two Royal Navy gunboats were launched for proposed use on the River Danube.

The company was founded by James Skinner, a former draughtsman with Leslie's yard at Hebburn, and William Wood, who had been a shipyard cashier. Production began c1884-85, with the firm employing over 600 men.

The most unusual product of Wood Skinner's Bill Quay yard was the Floating Fever Hospital, ordered by the Tyne Port Sanitary Authority. The hospital was completed in 1886 and moored at the entrance of Jarrow Slake to accommodate seamen arriving in the river with infectious diseases.

Vessels launched included the long-serving vehicle ferry *South Shields*, of 1911, which plied back and forth across the Tyne on the Shields Market Place route for an extraordinary 57 years. Like many others, the Wood Skinner yard suffered from the slump of the 1920s and closed in 1928. During the Second World War and afterwards radar equipment was manufactured on the site and in the 1980s it was occupied by Marconi Radar.

A nearby site at Bill Quay was the location of the wooden shipbuilding yard founded by William Boutland in c.1818. Boutland's three sons took over the business after his death in 1859 and the firm lasted until c.1880. Sailing vessels such as snows and schooners featured prominently in the output.

The southern bank of the Tyne also featured tug-builders J.P. Rennoldson & Sons, whose shipyard was situated in the East End of South Shields, below the Lawe Top. The yard probably occupied part of the old Wallis shipbuilding site. Founded in 1826 as marine engine builders, Rennoldson's began constructing and repairing wooden vessels in the 1860s. Iron shipbuilding started at the yard in the 1870s. The

J.P. Rennoldson's Yard at South Shields c.1914, situated below the Lawe Top. The yard became renowned for its output of tugs.

firm launched mainly tugs and some trawlers. By 1904 over 200 vessels had been produced. The output included the salvage tug *Lady Brassey*, of 1913, launched for the Dover Harbour Board. She put in fine service during both world wars and took part in around 200 salvage operations.

J.P. Rennoldson's last craft was probably the powerful twin-screw tug *Atlas*, launched in 1926 for service on the Suez Canal. Afterwards, orders seem to have dried up and within a couple of years the business collapsed.

The firm had been run for 35 years by two brothers, Charles and Joseph, sons of James Purdy Rennoldson. However, in 1913 the partnership was dissolved and the following year Charles opened a separate shipbuilding yard on land next to his brother's, below the Lawe Top, but a little closer to the Groyne. This was known appropriately as the Lawe Shipyard. The first craft from Charles Rennoldson's

A proud moment recorded in the Smith's Dock Journal. The men who repaired the benzine carrier Patella *of the Anglo Saxon Petroleum Company in 1921, pose for a picture at Smith's Dock, North Shields. One of the conditions of the contract was that the job of repairing collision damage to this ship should be completed within 16 working days. The job was finished two days early.*

new base were two salvage vessels for the Mersey Docks & Harbour Board. During the First World War the firm was engaged on Admiralty work, including the construction of a minesweeping sloop. After the conflict, the output included trawlers.

Charles was said to have treated his workmen well and he was evidently a popular employer. His death in 1924 was a considerable blow. By the spring of 1926 the yard had closed. The site today is occupied by the Littlehaven housing development and was formerly the site of Velva Liquids' storage tanks.

One of J.P Rennoldson's major rivals in tug-building was the firm of J.T. Eltringham, which was founded by Joseph Eltringham and Thomas Toward at South Shields in 1846. Initially building boilers and tanks, a shipyard was developed from 1864. The yard was located between the Middle Docks area and Mill Dam on a site known as the Stone Quay, just a short distance above Mill Dam. During its many years at South Shields the firm launched well over 200 small vessels and gained a

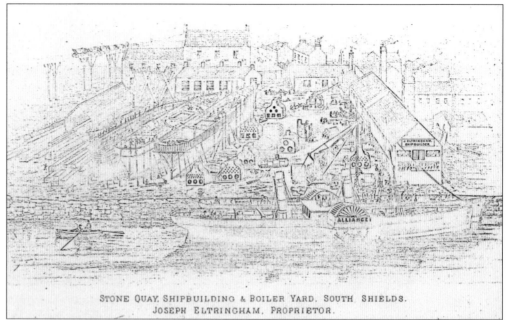

STONE QUAY, SHIPBUILDING & BOILER YARD, SOUTH SHIELDS.
JOSEPH ELTRINGHAM, PROPRIETOR.

Top, an early drawing of Eltringham's yard at the Stone Quay, South Shields, a short distance up river from Mill Dam.
Below, Eltringham's Yard at Howdon in c1914.

worldwide reputation for craft such as trawlers and tenders, as well as screw and paddle tugs. In 1878, Eltringham's built what was thought to be the first iron steam trawler. Its tug, *Old Trafford*, of 1907, is preserved in the National Maritime Museum under her later name *Reliant*.

The year 1912 saw the firm acquire Palmers' Howdon Yard and all operations were transferred there from South Shields in 1913-14. Like many others, the company was hit by the slump following the First World War and in 1932 the yard closed. This was said to be a temporary measure. However, the gates of Eltringham's at Howdon never reopened.

Another example of a prominent Tyne tug-builder was the firm of Hepple, which was set up c.1862. Its first recorded site is now occupied by A. & P. Tyne's Wallsend dry docks. In later years, Hepple's moved to North Shields and then to a site at Wapping Street in South Shields in c1902. Hepple's produced many paddle tugs as well as other craft. Its South Shields yard lasted until 1924.

The northern bank, at Wallsend, was the site of the Schlesinger Davis shipyard. This firm was set up in 1863 by Charles Schlesinger, who had trained at Stephenson's Works in Newcastle, and Frederick Davis, who trained with Charles Mitchell at Low Walker.

Their first two vessels were sailing ships and these were followed, in 1864, by their first steamer, the *Llandaff*. Many other steamers followed. The yard closed in 1893 after 30 years of production and in 1897 the land was acquired by the neighbouring company of C.S. Swan & Hunter. The Schlesinger Davis site thus became part of Swan Hunter's Wallsend Shipyard. In the 1980s, during a clear-out of the old drawing office at Swan Hunter, a cylindrical slide rule calcu-

WALLSEND.

Schlesinger, Davis, & Co.

IRON AND STEEL

SHIP BUILDERS.

ALL DESCRIPTIONS OF STEAM OR SAILING VESSELS, YACHTS, TUG BOATS, LAUNCHES, DREDGERS, &c., BUILT IN EITHER IRON OR STEEL.

WALLSEND,

NEWCASTLE-ON-TYNE

An advertisement for the Schlesinger Davis yard at Wallsend. It was later incorporated into C.S. Swan and Hunter's Wallsend Yard.

lator was discovered in a box. The box and an accompanying instruction book were clearly marked with the Schlesinger Davis rubber stamp. It was an extraordinary survival from an earlier era of shipbuilding. The slide rule calculator is today in the care of Newcastle Discovery Museum.

In 1919-20 a shipyard was laid out at Hebburn immediately to the west of the Hawthorn Leslie site. The business formed to run it was the Newcastle Shipbuilding Co. Ltd. A ship named the *Zabalbide* was launched for a Spanish company in December 1920. A second ship was then launched, the *Ravnefjell*. However, the Newcastle Shipbuilding Co was soon engulfed by a financial crisis and in April 1921 it was decided to close the business down. The *Zabalbide* was towed away and completed by another firm at Hartlepool. The *Ravnefjell* was completed in Scotland.

The river has indeed seen many closures, but of all the Tyne's yards the most unlucky was that set up by Newcastle businessmen Sir George Renwick, a former MP, and R.S. Dalgleish, a city councillor. In 1918, they acquired a site at Hebburn between Jarrow Staith and Palmers' Hebburn Yard. Two years later, Renwick and Dalgleish submitted plans to the Tyne Improvement Commission for a concrete jetty, riverside wall and six building berths. The commission duly approved the scheme and work began on the project.

Although it seems that four of the six berths were completed, the yard was unable to obtain any orders because of the slump in the industry. Almost inevitably, the site was acquired by National Shipbuilders Security Ltd in 1931 and its plant and machinery auctioned off. The Renwick and Dalgleish yard had closed without launching a single ship. Sir George Renwick died in the same year, aged 81. His five sons

A gift to Newcastle. The Renwick Memorial beside St Thomas's Church, Haymarket, paid for by Sir George Renwick and his wife. Sir George's shipbuilding venture on the banks of the Tyne proved to be a disaster.

had returned safely from the First World War and in appreciation of this happy event he and his wife gave the superb war memorial at Barras Bridge, Newcastle, to the city.

The work of Sir W. Goscombe John, R.A., the memorial is set amid floral displays next to the Civic Centre and St Thomas's Church and is called *The Response*. It portrays in bronze and stone men volunteering for military service at the start of the First World War in 1914. The finely-modelled figures also include women and children bidding farewell to their loved ones in a moving tribute of great emotional power. The memorial commemorates the raising of several volunteer battalions of the Northumberland Fusiliers.

Perhaps Sir George Renwick is best remembered for his kind gift of this beautiful memorial to Newcastle rather than his ill-fated shipbuilding venture on the banks of the Tyne.

A Cascade of Buzzers

O ver a period of 200 or more years many small yards have come and gone on the Tyne, some lasting only a short time. However, a few of the smaller yards, specialising in vessels of modest dimensions, survived for a long period. Among these was Cleland's, of Willington Quay.

William Cleland, the founder of the yard, was, like John Coutts, Charles Mitchell and Andrew Leslie, a Scot. He had been manager of Palmers' Howdon Yard, but in 1867 set up his own shiprepair business on nearby land at Willington Quay, using a 600ft-long slipway which the firm claimed was the best in the North of England.

William died in 1876, aged 54, but his sons and a brother seem to have carried on the family connection with the business. In c.1897 the company began building small steel vessels, including trawlers, but repair work remained a leading element of the business.

The firm lived on into the 20th century, and then the Depression of the early 1930s hit Cleland's hard. In 1934 the yard was sold to Yorkshire firm Craggs of Goole for only £3,000. The Craggs era was to see many changes. Cleland's was gradually modernised and became well known for turning out a wide variety of small craft, including coasters, barges, river ferries, lifting vessels, deep-freeze trawlers and large tugs. In 1960 the yard built the *Suvretta*, a palatial motor yacht, a departure from its more usual mundane orders.

John Dobson

The coaster Quiescence *of Rochester shortly before her launch at Cleland's Yard, Willington Quay, in December 1958.*

Photo supplied courtesy of the Shields Gazette

John Dobson, of Cochrane Park, Newcastle, served as an apprentice fitter at Cleland's from 1956 to 1961. It seems that the working hours in the Tyne yards had not changed a great deal since the 1940s. John remembers starting at 7.30am and finishing at 5.15pm.

He tells of the buzzer which sounded out at the start and finish of the working day and which also marked the dinner hour. 'All the buzzers or hooters of the shipyards along the Tyne used to go off at about the same time, although because they were all on different clocks they were rarely exactly simultaneous. It was a cascade of buzzers.'

Shortly after he started at the yard in 1956, John was given the honour of presenting a bouquet to a young lady who launched a ship at Cleland's. 'I was 15-and-a-half and she was 16, so we were virtually the same age. I got £1 for carrying out this little duty, which to an apprentice in those days was a large sum of money.'

Apprentice John Dobson, aged 15, presents a bouquet to 16-year-old Annabelle Jenkin before she launches the cargo vessel Heathergate *14 November 1956.*

The young lady was Annabelle Jenkin, a relation of one of the shipping company's owners. The vessel she launched was the *Heathergate*, a small cargo carrier.

'I remember I had to go home and get changed into my Sunday suit for the ceremony. When I tried to get back into the yard they didn't recognise me at first because I was usually dressed in a boiler suit.'

Cleland's had sideways launching berths as well as con- ventional ones and John remembers two small coasters being launched sideways into Willington Gut, a tributary of the Tyne, rather than the Tyne itself. Other launches using this method included a pair of large tugs built for service in the Gulf.

The yard was probably one of the last on the Tyne to use a 'board' system of recording timekeeping rather than the more usual clocking in and off. The 'boards' were small pieces of wood with a man's works number on top. Each man would record in pencil on his board when he started work and when he finished as well as what ship or contract he was working on that day. The board had to be signed or initialled by a chargehand.

Of his time at Cleland's, John says: 'It is sometimes said that schooldays are the happiest of your life. To me, this was not the case. Some of my happiest days were at the shipyard. It was a fascinating place to work'

The company became part of the Swan Hunter group in 1967, later joining the small ship division of British Shipbuilders during the period of nationalisation. Cleland's closed in 1984. Its site was the first yard to the east of Willington Gut.

Down river and immediately east of the Cleland's location is the land once occupied by the Tyne Iron Shipbuilding Company. This business was set up by William Bone, who had worked as a yard manager, in 1876. By 1889 the site, which became known as the Tyne Iron Yard, was employing around 800 men.

Building mainly small cargo ships, it survived into the 20th century and in 1914 launched the first twin-screw diesel engined ship constructed on the Tyne, the *Elbruz*. The company suffered in the post-First World War slump like many others and in 1921 built only two vessels. The business foundered in 1928 and was taken over by Armstrong Whitworth. A few more ships were built at the yard, but by 1931 there were no more orders. In 1933 the Tyne Iron Yard

Workmen in the early 1900s at the Mercantile Dry Dock, Jarrow, which began operating in 1889. The yard specialised for many years in the repair of tramp steamers and other small vessels.

was sold to National Shipbuilders Security Ltd for dismantling.

Further to the east again is the location of the former Palmers' Howdon yard, later to be taken over by tug-builders J.T. Eltringham, and to the east of this, down river, the site of the Tyne Improvement Commission's former workshops and repair yard, once the location of 18th century wooden shipbuilder Francis Hurry.

Down river further is the land which was occupied by the

Northumberland Shipbuilding Company. This business was founded by Rowland Hodge, another experienced manager, in 1898. He took over the Edwards yard, which was next to the Northumberland Dock, and modernised it, creating five berths, which were later increased to seven. The first ship launched was the *Ravenshoe*, in 1899.

On December 23 1908 a Greek steamer, the *Patris,* was launched from the yard, but the drag chains parted and the out-of-control vessel moved rapidly across the river, crashing through the gates of No. 1 dry dock at the Mercantile Dry Dock, Jarrow. The *Patris* collided with the stern of a ship named the *Ilderton,* causing considerable damage to both vessels.

Fortunately, there were no men inside the dock as the *Ilderton* was in the process of being re-floated prior to undocking. It was also fortunate the *Patris* did not hit the gates of No. 2 dock where a large gang of men were working.

However, across the river in the shipyard a carpenter was injured when the first drag chain parted. He was taken to the Tynemouth Victoria Jubilee Infirmary after being struck in the chest by a shackle.

The *Patris* remained trapped on the sill of the dry dock for about an hour, but was then towed free by six tugs. The incident did not prevent the management and guests of the shipyard from celebrating the launch. A meal was served in the mould loft and a toast drunk to the 'success of the *Patris*'.

During the First World War the Northumberland Shipbuilding Company pioneered 'standard' ship types. These were cargo vessels built to a single design which could be quickly constructed to carry vital food and supplies. Indeed, in 1918, near the end of the war, the yard claimed the record for the fastest completion of a vessel, the 'standard' steamer *War Citadel,* designed by managing director Rowland Hodge. She was launched on November 4 of that year and on November 7, at 9am, the engines were steamed. The vessel was handed over to the owners in the afternoon.

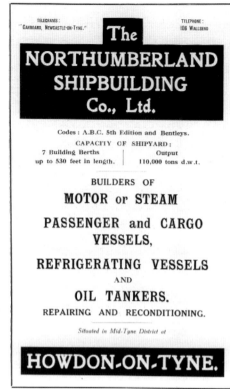

The company collapsed in 1926 but was revived the following year under the name Northumberland Shipbuilding Company (1927) Ltd. However, the Depression of the early 1930s brought about its downfall and, like the Tyne Iron Yard, it was sold to National Shipbuilders Security Ltd for dismantling.

In more recent times the sites of Cleland's, the Tyne Iron Shipbuilding Company, Palmers' Howdon Yard and the Northumberland Shipbuilding Company were used by Press Offshore for oil rig module building.

Up river, at Walker, is the site of the former Dobson's yard, which was set up in 1883 by William Dobson, who had been a manager with Mitchell's Low Walker Yard. He was also a Scot and worked in shipbuilding on the Clyde before coming to the Tyne. The location of Dobson's yard was off Wincomblee Road, between Mitchell's Low Walker Yard and the land which would become the site of the Walker Naval Yard. Dobson's had three berths for vessels up to 10,000 tons and a smaller berth for craft such as tugs and hopper barges. The firm was prepared to build a wide variety of river and coastal vessels. Its output also included a considerable number of small cargo ships for Hall Brothers of Newcastle.

But like so many others, the 1920s slump brought problems for the business and the company was acquired by Armstrong Whitworth in 1928. Dobson's was sold in 1934 to National Shipbuilders Security Ltd and its plant and machinery auctioned off the following year. The Second World War briefly revived both the Dobson and Mitchell sites when the Shipbuilding Corporation, a wartime creation, built cargo vessels and other craft there. After the war, Dobson's closed again, its berths and workshops falling silent for the final time.

We have seen that the Elswick Shipyard of Armstrong Whitworth was situated 11 miles from the sea, but intriguingly it was not the furthest yard up river. A business known as Campbell, Mackintosh and Bowstead began building vessels on a site at Scotswood, immediately to the east of the old Scotswood Suspension Bridge, around 1880. Its yard was located in part of the area now occupied by the Alvis Vickers factory. This company built 18 ships.

Later the yard was occupied by the firm of Campbell,

Bowstead, which seems to have been the previous business in a new form without Mackintosh. In 1891 another business took over the yard, the Scotswood Shipbuilding Company. Vessels launched by this firm included the *Helios* and *Triton*. These were paddle steamers designed to carry passengers on the River Plate in South America. They were based at Montevideo, capital of Uruguay. The managing director was Thomas Elsee who had Uruguayan connections and seems to have had a home there. It may well be that the firm was founded mainly to build ships for South American coastal and river services.

The Scotswood Shipbuilding Company did not, however, last long. The yard, probably the furthest from the sea of any other shipbuilders on the Tyne, closed around 1895 following a disastrous fire the previous year. In 1899 the site was purchased by Armstrong Whitworth for an extension to their Scotswood Works. The Scotswood Shipbuilding Company had vanished into history.

Industrial Hobos

George Andrews, from Elswick, Newcastle, served an apprenticeship at the Elswick Works as a fitter and turner, but he wanted to join the Merchant Navy and become a marine engineer. He writes: 'After completing my apprenticeship at the age of 22 in 1949 I joined the Walker Naval Yard to get marine engineering experience.

'In my trade when work was slack we could be paid off at 24 hours' notice. This was not a problem, however, as the best part of the workforce was classed as 'floating labour' and we would travel to various yards up and down the Tyne to where the work for our respective trades was available. We called ourselves 'industrial hobos.'

'Just after the Second World War a fitter's wage was £7 per week for 47 hours worked and there was plenty of over-time. The average tradesman could earn about £12 per week, which was a very good wage in 1949.

'Most shipyards paid their workforce on Friday at 5.15pm when we had to stand in a long queue in numerical order. The wages were brought to the various departments, or cab-ins on the jetty, for the outfitting trades, and we were paid by our departmental time clerks.'

The men received their pay in cash. 'If there were any mistakes in wages, we had to wait until the next week to get them put right.'

He recalls there were problems at times getting to work. 'I can remember in the 1950s when the old trolley buses trav-elled down to Walker and Wallsend. The fare was 4d to Walker and 5d to Wallsend from the West End of Newcastle.

'We could usually time the bus in the morning to get into the Wallsend Yard from 7.30 which was our starting time, but there were often power cuts in the early 50s and buses would be stopped in their tracks. It seemed to always happen when the buses were some distance from the shipyard, which meant we had to get off and walk the rest of the way and lose time.' This, of course, meant that George and his workmates would lose money.

Of the hazards, George writes: 'The shipyards were very dangerous places. We had to keep watch wherever we went aboard a ship as the lighting wasn't too good in the early stages of construction.

'After the laying of a ship's keel, bulkhead frames and shellplates were erected first. The installation of steam and oil pipes, sea-valves and auxiliaries were ongoing at the same time. The assembly of the main engine and the boilers fol-lowed. The electrical wiring was in progress at this time, and the construction of the cabins and other woodwork followed.

'After the boilers, main steam pipes and valves had been assembled the insulating men would cover the steam pipes and boilers with asbestos lagging to contain the heat when the steam was produced. Asbestos dust spread throughout the working area in which it was being handled.'

It proved to be a serious danger to health and many years

Two ships at the Wallsend Dry Docks of Swan Hunter c.1946. This major ship repair base is today operated by A. & P. Tyne. The well-known landmark of St Andrew's Church, Hebburn, is top left. The docks were founded by the Tyne Pontoons & Dry Dock Company, opening in 1887. The company was absorbed by Swan Hunter in 1903.

later former shipyard men have developed mesothelioma, a malignant tumour of the lung lining, as a result of their exposure to this hazardous material. In 2004 it was reported that about 125 people in the North-East were dying every year as a result of mesothelioma. The majority were men who had worked in the region's shipyards in the 1950s, 60s and 70s.

The condition, a form of lung cancer directly linked to asbestos exposure, can take many years to develop. Medical experts estimated that the number of cases would peak in 2015 to 2020. The use of asbestos as a building material is now banned.

Among the other hazards in many shipyards as late as the 1950s and 1960s was the lack of protective headgear. 'We had to make sure no one was working above us, as we had no helmets during the early years,' George says. 'A lot of us just wore our cloth caps.'

There were other problems too, though less serious. 'On many occasions in the early days we practically had to use sign language to communicate with each other, as the noise from the caulkers and riveters was deafening. We also had to watch our eyes for welder's flash, which gives a sensation of having a lot of sand in your eyes. This meant a trip to the medical centre to get special drops put in our eyes to relieve the irritation.

'In winter, with thousands of tonnes of steel around, it was bitterly cold. There were riveters' fires at various places and a lot of the men used to warm themselves at intervals and make cans of tea.'

George and his friends also worked in the shiprepair yards at various times. 'We learned through the grapevine or

Shipping Gazette when repair jobs were coming into the Tyne. 'Hobos' like myself used to go for the repair work as our wages could rise by about one third.

'In those days the shiprepair industry had a market place system of recruiting their labour force. Men needing work used to come into a yard before 7.30am dressed in their working clothes and stand until the foreman came out of his office. If selected they would be started immediately.'

Shiprepair has been an important industry on the river for centuries. South Shields in particular was a natural stronghold of this activity since Shields Harbour was the first place reached by vessels entering the river in need of mending.

By the early 20th Century major repair firms such as Brigham & Cowan, Tyne Dock Engineering and Middle Dock lined the South Shields riverside.

Brigham & Cowan was founded in 1874 and for a number of years was based near Middle Dock. However, in 1905 it began operating from new premises in Wapping Street where a large dry dock had been installed. The site was further expanded in 1924 when Hepple's yard, immediately up river, closed and was absorbed into the complex.

The Middle Dock and Engineering Company was set up in 1899, although its site between Readhead's yard and Mill Dam had long been used for shipbuilding and repair. The original Middle Dock was installed some time between 1765 and 1768 and later a second dock was added. The new Middle Dock & Engineering Company of 1899 added two more docks. The largest of these, opened in early 1917, was 630ft long and occupied part of the old Eltringham's site, almost immediately up river from Mill Dam. During the Second World War this dock was lengthened to 640ft so that

The British India Line cargo vessel Woodarra *in the newly built No. 4 dry dock at the Mercantile Dry Dock, Jarrow, in 1961. She was one of the first ships to use the new facility.*

heavy cruisers could be accommodated.

Tyne Dock Engineering (known as TDE) was situated near the Market Place ferry landing and was another important shiprepair concern. Its history stretched back to the 19th Century when it was located near Tyne Dock. A TDE joint stock company was formed in 1889 to acquire the Market Dock, almost immediately down river from the Market Place ferry landing and the Alum House. This site, which had been used by Simon Temple Junior, became the company's new home.

The skills of these three South Shields firms played a major role in both world wars, their workmen being kept constantly occupied repairing damaged naval vessels and merchant ships.

During the First World War teams of men from leading Tyne shiprepair firms, including those of South Shields, did spells of duty patching up warships at the Tyne-built Admiralty Floating Dock moored off Jarrow Slake.

The Second World War saw both Brigham & Cowan and TDE damaged by German bombing raids in 1941.

The Mercantile Dry Dock at Jarrow and Palmers' Hebburn Yard were also important centres kept busy by the constant need to mend, maintain and refit countless vessels vital to the world's trade.

The Mercantile Dry Dock Company, which occupied a site a short distance down river from Palmers Jarrow Yard, opened its first dock in 1889, which had been installed on the site of a ballast hill. Two more docks were added in later years. This shiprepair firm handled numerous tramp steamers and colliers. A fourth, much larger

The Armstrong Whitworth Russian icebreaker Yermack *(sometimes written* Ermack*) in the ice. She returned to the Tyne in 1905 for repairs at the Hebburn Dry Dock of Robert Stephenson after she was damaged in the White Sea. Photograph by Parry.*

dock was opened at the yard in 1961 and this enabled the company to handle ships such as tankers. In addition, British India Line vessels were among those coming in for repair and maintenance. The Mercantile Dry Docks closed in 1981.

However, the largest dry dock on the North-East Coast was the 700ft-long giant at Palmers' Hebburn yard. This dock had been completed in 1904 by the famous Newcastle locomotive-building firm of Robert Stephenson, which operated the yard before its takeover by Palmers in 1911-12. Stephenson's built a considerable number of vessels at Hebburn, but its huge dry dock seems to have attracted much more attention. It was soon busy handling important ships. In October 1905, for instance, Armstrong Whitworth's Russian icebreaker *Yermack* was docked for repairs after her shell plating was damaged when she ran aground while convoying vessels in the White Sea to the mouth of the River Yenesei. *Yermack* had gone ashore during fog near Archangel. Extensive repairs were carried out in the dock over several weeks and a new cast steel rudder fitted.

Immediately following the undocking of this icebreaker in late November 1905, the large Hawthorn Leslie-built Russian Volunteer cruiser *Smolensk* was docked for extensive bottom repairs. This work lasted until early February 1906. After the *Smolensk*, it was the turn of Armstrong Whitworth's Japanese battleship *Kashima* to enter the dry dock. The Elswick-built *Kashima* was painted and her fitting completed prior to sea trials. By July 1906, the dock's workmen were beginning repairs to the *Narragansett*, then the world's largest oil tanker.

Smaller ships were, of course, the bread-and-butter work of more modest-sized repair yards. One of the longest-lasting of the smaller repair firms was R.B. Harrison & Son, of Bill Quay, founded in the 19th century. The business moved from St Anthony's, Newcastle, on the northern bank to its site at Bill Quay on the southern shore in c.1899, occupying the river frontage of the former Boutland's wooden yard. Harrison's specialised in the repair of smaller craft, such as fishing boats and tugs. They also built a number of modest-sized vessels. The yard survived until the 1990s. At the time of writing, the site, near the Albion Inn, is derelict.

Another small firm which lasted many years was J & D Morris, whose yard was situated at Pelaw Main, a short distance down river from Harrison's, about half way between Bill Quay and Hebburn Quay. The business was set up by twins John and David Morris in 1847 and lasted until 1928. The yard carried out mainly shiprepair, but also built small

Harrison's Yard, Bill Quay, photographed in 1986. Both slipways are empty, but there is work alongside the yard.

vessels intermittently over it 80 or so years of existence. J & D Morris are believed to have launched more than 70 craft, and secured a number of Admiralty contracts during the First World War. In 1918-23, a series of small coasters were built by this family firm.

A site on the southern bank of the Tyne at Friar's Goose, Gateshead, was the location of T. Mitchison's small shiprepair yard. Mitchison bought the yard in 1919. In the 1830s this site was occupied by a wooden shipbuilding yard. Later, it became a repair facility known as Anderson's Slipway.

T. Mitchison's occupation of the yard lasted until 1955 and they specialised in the repair of small vessels such as tugs. The company advertised itself as having a slipway for vessels up to 230ft long and a repairing quay. In 1955 the yard was taken over by the London-based firm of James Burness & Sons who built a number of modest-sized vessels there, including trawlers, until 1964. Sideways launchings were a feature of this yard.

The northern side of the river too had its yards specialising in repair, with Smith's Dock at North Shields handling countless ships. In addition, several major shipbuilders operated their own repair departments. For example, Swan Hunter & Wigham Richardson owned the Wallsend Dry Docks, which are still in the business of shiprepair today under the ownership of A. & P. Tyne, and Readhead's and Hawthorn Leslie were also well aware of the importance of this side of their activities. Repair work helped them to survive recessions in building. George Andrew's career mirrored yards such as these, he was both a builder and repairer. However, he did try lathe work in factories. But his heart was

in the yards with the ships and his friends, despite the dangerous and unpleasant conditions. Humour and camaraderie helped men to weather the difficulties and risks. Friendships were forged amid adversity. 'I always wanted to get back into the yards after a while because I missed the comradeship of my shipyard workmates, plus you could earn more money of course.'

George is not alone in his sentiments. The comradeship of the Tyne's yards is warmly remembered by many former workers. In addition, a man would often find himself working close to members of his family. Indeed, families with strong shipbuilding and shiprepair links can be found in abundance throughout Tyneside. Sons followed fathers, brothers, uncles and grandfathers into the yards. The histories of the river, its people and ships are inextricably intertwined.

But this great industry upon which so many livelihoods depended was subject to recessions as well as booms. The lean years brought unemployment. In contrast, during the better years customers worldwide flocked to the Tyne in the knowledge they would receive soundly-built vessels. The river's yards were also versatile. They could deliver ships of almost any type, although merchant vessels proved to be the mainstay of the order books.

Following the First World War there was a short-lived boom in orders from 1919-20, but by the end of 1923 the number of launchings had fallen considerably.

At the end of 1918 there were around 20 shipbuilding yards of various sizes on the Tyne. Fourteen of these would disappear before the advent of the Second World War in 1939. Most were taken over by National Shipbuilders

Smith's Dock featured pontoon docks as well as dry docks. This photograph shows the opening of No. 8 pontoon dock at North Shields in September 1892. It was evidently regarded as an occasion worth celebrating. Note the ships dressed overall in bunting. The large Smith's repair complex at North Shields handled countless vessels. Photograph by Parry.

Security Ltd with the aim of reducing 'over-capacity' in the industry from c.1928-1934. These unlucky yards were dismantled and their equipment sold off.

Those which survived were kept at full stretch during the Second World War. Following the conflict, the yards of Swan Hunter, Vickers-Armstrongs, Hawthorn Leslie and Readhead's remained the major shipbuilding sites on the Tyne. But all these yards, except Swan's at Wallsend, were destined to cease shipbuilding before the dawn of the 21st century.

The old company of Swan Hunter collapsed in 1993 and mass redundancies followed. However, in 1995 the Dutch-owned THC group purchased the Wallsend Shipyard for £5m. This eleventh-hour deal was struck only days before an auction of the yard's equipment was due to begin. Swan's had been in receivership for over two years.

A new company was formed to operate the yard, Swan Hunter (Tyneside) Ltd., headed by Dutch businessman Jaap Kroese, who thus saved shipbuilding on the Tyne from complete extinction for over a decade, provided much needed jobs and revived the training of apprentices.

Soon, the Wallsend Yard was stirring again. Under the leadership of Mr Kroese, the company converted the merchant ship *Solitaire* into the world's largest pipe-laying vessel. Then, late in 2000, the yard secured a deal to convert a tanker, *Global Producer,* into a floating oil production and storage vessel for the North Sea. Shortly afterwards, came the first order to build, rather than convert ships at the Wallsend Yard since the collapse of the old Swan's. This was for two Royal Fleet Auxiliary amphibious landing vessels, *Largs Bay* and *Lyme Bay*. Each ship was built within a float-

Largs Bay *under construction at Swan Hunter (Tyneside) Ltd, 2003.*

Swan Hunter (Tyneside) Ltd

ing dock placed with a specially excavated "inland harbour", similar to a dry dock but always containing water.

The vessels were launched by floating the dock out of the inland harbour and then sinking the dock into the Tyne until the ships became water-borne. *Largs Bay* was the first to be launched and was delivered in April 2006. Delays and escalating costs on the project led the Ministry of Defence to order that her sister ship, *Lyme Bay,* be towed from the Tyne to the Clyde for completion. She departed the yard in July 2006. Swan's had suffered from the design teething problems associated with being the lead yard for this class of vessel.

However, although the Government was understood to have made a verbal promise that it would give Swan's a major portion of the order to build two giant aircraft carriers for the Royal Navy, it failed to honour this promise. It was a great blow to Swan's and at the time of writing it looks as if the Wallsend Yard, the Tyne's last true shipbuilding base, will

MAURETANIA
New Quadruple Turbine
The Largest Vessel Afloat

33,200 Tons
68,000 Horse-Power
Length 790 Feet
Breadth 88 Feet
Depth 60 Ft. 6 In.
Speed 27 Knots

An artist's impression of the Tyne's greatest passenger liner, the Mauretania, *which was completed at Swan Hunter & Wigham Richardson's Wallsend Yard in 1907. The Wallsend Yard continues to operate as a shipbuilding base under a new owner and looks to the future with optimism.*

close.

The Wallsend Yard has over 130 years made an immense contribution to the Tyne's reputation for shipbuilding. Its most famous ship was the legendary Cunard passenger liner *Mauretania*, holder of the Blue Riband for the fastest Atlantic crossing for 22 years eastwards and 20 years westwards. Completed in 1907, the *Mauretania* was driven by powerful turbine engines built by the Wallsend Slipway & Engineering Company. She became a symbol of all that was best in Tyneside workmanship.

Other notable ships from the Wallsend Yard have included the Cunard passenger liner *Carpathia*, completed in 1903, which rescued the survivors of the *Titanic* disaster in 1912, the passenger-cargo liner *Dominion Monarch*, the largest diesel motor-driven vessel in the world when completed in 1939, and the elegant Norwegian passenger ship *Bergensfjord*, launched in 1955.

Cargo and cargo-passenger liners were once a mainstay of the order books of Swan's, with 30 being launched for the British India Line, 24 for the Ellerman Line and 22 for the Port Line. Oil tankers too were important in the firm's output, including eight supertankers. The first of these giant vessels, *Esso Northumbria*, caused great interest among the people of Tyneside when she was launched at the Wallsend Yard by Princess Anne in 1969.

Wallsend witnessed the launch of two other great vessels in the late 20th Century. These were the modern day aircraft carriers HMS *Illustrious* and HMS *Ark Royal*, completed in the 1980s.

The last ship from the old firm of Swan Hunter was the Type 23 Duke Class frigate HMS *Richmond*, completed in

The last order for the old Swan Hunter company, the Tyne ferry, Pride of the Tyne, *was lifted into the river in 1993.*

1994 while the company was in receivership.

The last order to be placed with the old company was for the Tyne ferry *Pride of the Tyne*, run by Nexus, which was lifted into the river at Wallsend by one of the firm's large cranes in 1993. As well as operating on the busy Shields ferry route, *Pride of the Tyne* also undertakes pleasure cruises along the river.

Many yards have come and gone, but they have left an indelible impression on all who worked in them. The creation of a ship requires design expertise, technical knowledge, high levels of skill and sheer hard work. The men of the Tyne's lost shipyards possessed these qualities in great measure. They were the unsung heroes of a dangerous industry and their great labours should never be forgotten.

Looking down the Tyne from Bill Quay, c.1960. The coaster Oakdene *of Sunderland is under repair at R.B. Harrison's shiprepair yard in the foreground, right. Across the river a tanker is ready for launch at the Walker Naval Yard. The 250-ton hammerhead crane is in the middle of the picture. In the distance are the cranes of Swan Hunter's Wallsend Dry Docks and Wallsend Shipyard. On the south side of the river there are colliers at Pelaw Main Staiths. A France Fenwick tug is alongside, bottom left. Photograph by H.S. Thorne.*

Firms and shipyard locations on the River Tyne

This list of firms or partnerships includes those named as shipbuilders at some time and place, on the River Tyne. It is not claimed to be comprehensive. Before around 1800 there were many shipbuilders who now are just names, such as Gothard, Lashley or Wrangham.

T. Adamson & Sons Willington Quay c.1853-1858

W. Adamson Willington Quay 1859-1864

Adamson & Pringle Willington Quay 1865-1867

R. Armstrong North Shore, Newcastle c. 1844-1845

Anderson, Johnson & Littlejohn St Lawrence, Newcastle c. 1891

Anderson Laverick St Lawrence, Newcastle 1891-1894

Armstrong, Mitchell Elswick & Low Walker 1883-1897

Armstrong Whitworth Elswick, Low Walker, High Walker 1897-1927

Vickers-Armstrongs High Walker 1927-1980

Bainbridge & Wilson Willington Quay 1864-1866

Barclay, Donald St Peters, Newcastle 1858-1860

Barnfather & Readhead Hebburn Quay 1843-1864

W.M. Boutland Bill Quay 1818-1880

Thos. & Robt. Brown Jarrow 1813-1833

Jonathan Brown South Shore, Gateshead 1813-1824

Thomas Brown Gateshead, Howdon 1831-1851

Wm Brown & Sons St Lawrence, Newcastle 1881-1891

Brodie & Maxwell Coble Dene, North Shields 1864-1878

Burdis North and South Shields 1866-1868

Luke B. Bushell South Shields 1840-1858

Campbell, Mackintosh & Bowstead Scotswood 1880-1886

Campbell, Bowstead Scotswood 1887-1888

Cole Brothers Willington Quay 1871-1876

Wm Cleland & Co. Willington Quay 1867-1984

Coulson, Cooke & Co. St Peter's & Wallsend 1871-1874

John Coutts Low Walker 1842-1848

Coutts & Parkinson Willington Quay 1849-1855

Wm Cunningham St Lawrence 1839-1860

Wm Dobson & Co. Walker 1883-1928

C.W. Dodgin & Co. North Shields 1869-1875

Alex Doeg Gateshead 1788-1816

H.S. Edwards South Shields ?-1883

Edwards, Sons & Craig East Howden 1883-1898

Edwards Brothers North Shields 1893-1899

J.T. Eltringham S Shields & Willington Quay 1846-1933

Ekless & Oliver Bill Quay 1847-1848

Esson & Walker East Jarrow 1841-1844

Irwin & Fairs Friars Goose, Felling Shore 1834-1871

Rich. Farrington North Shore, Newcastle c1810-1830

Robt. Fell Junior St Peters, Newcastle 1876

Foster, Renwick & Shotton South Shore, Gateshead Fini 1819

Hall, Hills & Fulton Nelson St, North Shore, Newcastle 1845-1865

George Fawcus Dortwick Street, North Shields 1854-1881

Gaddy & Lamb Tyne Main, Gateshead 1840-1883

Gaddy, Brown & Lamb Tyne Main, Gateshead pre-1840

Gray & Robson South Shore, Tyne Main 1815-1830

George & Robert Gray South Shore, Friars Goose 1818-1850

J. and J. Hair St Peter's, Newcastle 1845-1857

R B Harrison & Son St Anthony's Quay / Bill Quay 1892-1993

Robert Harrison North Shore, St Peter's etc 1820-1880

Headlam & Co. South Shore, Gateshead 1743-1807

T.S. Henzell Howdon on Tyne 1857-1860

Holt, Walker & Co. Dunkirk Place, Jarrow 1833-1834

George Huntley Heworth Shore, Felling Shore 1816-1829

William P Huntley Hebburn Quay 1881-1918

Hepple Low Walker, North Shields, South Shields c1862-1924

Hepple & Landells Low Walker 1851-1862

A. & R. Hopper Nelson St, North Shore, Newcastle 1823-1870

Wm B Hornby Willington Quay 1869-1871

Geo. C. Hutchinson St Lawrence, St Peter's 1860-1870

Messrs Hurry Howdon Dock 1759-1806

L. Kirkup St Peters, Newcastle 1857-1858

Andrew Leslie & Co. Hebburn Quay 1853-1884

R.W. Hawthorn Leslie Hebburn Quay 1885-1967

Laing Brothers North Shields 1854-1859

Thomas Lawson Salmons Quay, South Shields 1884-1888

Edward Lindsay St Lawrence, Newcastle 1862-1881

John Lindsey St Anthony's, Walker 1879-1916

Lindsey Brothers St Anthony's, Walker 1925-1948

Lancelot Liddle Jarrow Quay 1879-1884

McIntyre & Co. Hebburn Quay 1883-1886

T.D. Marshall Lawe, South Shields 1830-1859

Marshall Brothers Willington Quay 1861-1868

Thomas Metcalfe Dunkirk Place, Jarrow 1800-1850

Miller, Ravenhill Co. Low Walker 1850-1854

Charles Mitchell Co. Low Walker 1852-1882

T. Mitchison Ltd Friars Goose, Felling 1919-1963

J. & D. Morris Pelaw Main, Hebburn 1847-1928

Newcastle S.B. Co. Hebburn 1919-1921

Northumberland S.B. Co. East Howdon 1898-1931

Palmer S.B. & I Co. Jarrow, Hebburn, Howdon 1852-1933

H. Penman Whitehill Point, North Shields 1870-1876

Cuthbert Potts St Anthony's, Walker 1825-1860

Thomas Potts St Anthony's Walker 1846-1859

Readhead & Softley Lawe, South Shields 1865-1872

John Readhead & Sons West Docks, South Shields 1872-1968

J.P. Rennoldson & Sons Lawe, South Shields 1826-1926

Charles Rennoldson Lawe, South Shields 1913-1930

A launch postcard for an unknown ship, 1914, shows building berths at the Charles Rennoldson Yard at the Lawe, South Shields.

Rennison Heworth Shore, Bill Quay 1824-1858

Oliver & Spoor Mill Dam, South Shields 1845-1860

Renwick & Dalgliesh Hebburn 1918-1931

William Reay Walker Quay 1831-1842

Messrs Rogerson & Co. St Peter's, Newcastle 1855-1864

Jonathan Robson Blackwall, South Shore, Gateshead 1830-1862

William Rowe St Peter's, Newcastle 1756-1810

David C. Ross Jarrow Quay 1858-1861

Ryton Marine Ltd Davy Bank, Wallsend 1971-1975

Scotswood S.B. Co. Scotswood, Newcastle 1891-1895

Schlesinger, Davis & Co. Wallsend 1863-1893

George K. Smith Whitehill Point, N Shields 1882-1883

Thompson & Chas Smith Willington Quay 1835-1851

J. Stevenson, Stephenson St Anthony's 1814-1841

T. & W. Smith St Peter's & North Shields 1810-1892

Thomas Seymour Low Walker, Newcastle 1848-1852

John Softley Lawe, South Shields 1872-1875

John Softley & Sons South Shields 1877-1880

Thomas Sopwith St Anthony's 1845

Richard Stobbs Coble Dene, North Shields 1854-1895

D.T. Stewart Coble Dene, North Shields 1866-1870

Robert Stephenson & Co. Hebburn 1887-1910

Straker & Love Howdon Dock 1840-1846

C.S. Swan & Co. Wallsend 1874-1880

C.S. Swan & Hunter Wallsend 1880-1903

Swan, Hunter & Wigham Richardson Wallsend 1903-1968

Swan Hunter & Tyne Shipbuilders Mid-Tyne 1968-1986

Swan Hunter Wallsend 1986-1994

Swan Hunter (Tyneside) Ltd Wallsend 1995-

Tyne General Ferry Co. St Peter's 1881-1891

Simon Temple (Snr & Jnr) Jarrow 1780-1813

William Trenholm Coble Dene, North Shields 1849

Thomas Toward St Peter's, Newcastle 1840-1854

T. & W. Toward Low Benwell, Newcastle 1882-1884

Robert Trotter Bill Quay, Howdon & Jarrow 1840-1861

Tyne Iron S.B. Co. Willington Quay 1876-1928

Tyne Iron S.B. Co. St Peter's, Newcastle 1864-1871

William Torrance Hebburn, Walker & Bill Quay 1835-1881

Robert Wallis Lawe, South Shields c1729-1780

Wouldhave & Johnson North Shields 1879-1885

John Vernon Low Walker 1854-1857

J. Wigham Richardson Neptune Yard, Walker 1860-1903

J.W. Wilkinson St Anthony's 1839-1860

Wood, Skinner & Co. Bill Quay 1883-1928

J. Winlo & Co. Howdon, Jarrow, South Shields 1839-1894

Young(s) South Shields 1819-1871

Index of names and ships